Ethical Child Welfare Practice

University of Chicago School of Social Service Administration

Office of the Inspector General, Illinois Department of Children and Family Services

Martin Leever

Gina DeCiani

Ellen Mulaney

Heather Hasslinger

In conjunction with:

Eileen Gambrill

Supervised by:

Denise Kane

Elsie Pinkston

CWLA Press • Washington, DC

CWLA Press is an imprint of the Child Welfare League of America. The Child Welfare League of America is the nation's oldest and largest membership-based child welfare organization. We are committed to engaging people everywhere in promoting the well-being of children, youth, and their families, and protecting every child from harm.

CHILD WELFARE LEAGUE OF AMERICA, INC.
HEADQUARTERS
440 First Street, NW, Third Floor, Washington, DC 20001-2085
E-mail: books@cwla.org

CURRENT PRINTING (last digit)
10 9 8 7 6 5 4 3 2 1

Cover design by Michael T. Rae
Text design by Mary Flannery and Tegan A. Culler

Printed in the United States of America

ISBN # 0-87868-819-6

Library of Congress Cataloging-in-Publication Data

Ethical Child Welfare Practice / by the University of Chicago School of Social Service Administration, the Office of the Inspector General of the Department of Children and Family Services, State of Illinois; [Martin Leever ... et al.].
    p. cm.
  Includes bibliographical references.
  ISBN 0-87868-819-6
    1. Child welfare--moral and ethical aspects. I. Leever, Martin. II. University of Chicago. School of Social Service Administration. III. Illinois Dept. of Children and Family Services. office of Inspector General.

HV715 .E842002
362.7--dc21   2001043244

Acknowledgements

The Illinois Department of Children and Family Services appreciates the many staff members with the Office of the Inspector General who assisted in the preparation of this publication and provided helpful examples and discussion on various issues.

A special debt of gratitude is also owed to the Child Welfare Ethics Advisory Board for reviewing and providing critical feedback on the content of the manual: Commander Roberta Bartik, J.D., Chicago Police Department; Michael Bennett, Ph.D., Director, Msgr. John J. Egan Urban Center, DePaul University; Dorothy Carpenter, M.Ed., Chicago Housing Authority; Michael Davis, Ph.D., Center for the Study of Ethics in the Professions, Illinois Institute of Technology; Esther Jenkins, Ph.D., Chicago State University; Phyllis Johnson, Ph.D., Illinois Department of Children and Family Services; Anthony Marchlewski, M.D., Great Lakes Psychiatric Center; David Ozar, Ph.D., Director, Center for Ethics, Loyola University of Chicago; Ada Skyles, Ph.D., J.D., Chapin Hall Center for Children, University of Chicago; and Gene Svebakken, M.S.W., Executive Director and C.E.O. Lutheran Child and Family Services

Also providing useful comments were Harold Bernt, ACSW, Director of Program Services, Metropolitan Family Services; Jim Lago, M.S.W., Executive Director, Catholic Charities of the Archdiocese of Chicago; John Schnier, M.S.W., Associate Executive Director, Lutheran Social Services of Illinois; and Cleo Terry, M.S.W., Vice-President, Child and Family Services, Lifelink-Bensenville Home Society.

We thank Arlene Gruber, M.S.W., M.A., for her work in organizing and shaping the OIG Ethics program in its early years.

Contents

Tables

Figure

Introduction

In 1996, the Illinois Department of Children and Family Services (DCFS) adopted the *Code of Ethics for Child Welfare Professionals*. The *Code* provides ethical guidelines for child welfare workers, supervisors, and administrators and sets out the values underlying the child welfare profession in summary form. Following the development of the Code, DCFS developed *Ethical Child Welfare Practice: A Companion Handbook for the Code of Ethics for Child Welfare Professionals* to explain in a reader-friendly fashion the ethical principles in more detail, and to illustrate them with examples. The handbook also described methods for analyzing practice dilemmas when ethical principles conflict. Copies of the Code and the Handbook may be obtained from the Office of the Inspector General, 2240 W. Ogden Ave., Chicago, IL 60612; telephone: 312/433-3000.

This publication is based on the *Code* and the *Handbook* and is designed to provide child welfare professionals with a framework for assessing ethical dilemmas, making sound ethical decisions, and delivering services with integrity to clients. It is the first of two planned volumes. This volume is focused on clinical issues and the provision of direct services to child welfare clients. A second volume will address ethical issues that pertain to the particular responsibilities of child welfare administrators. Although this publication and the volume planned to follow are designed to assist individual caseworkers and administrators improve their ethical decisionmaking ability, such decisionmaking is best conducted as a team effort. When faced with decisions of great magnitude, caseworkers, supervisors, and ethics staff should work together.

By developing ethical decisionmaking skills, child welfare professionals can improve the quality and integrity of the services they provide. Ethical decisionmaking skills also provide a tool that child welfare caseworkers, supervisors, and agencies can use to protect themselves from professional liability. Because the law can be ambiguous in many of the complex situations that arise in child welfare, decisions can be controversial. Child welfare professionals can make the best decisions and, at the same time, protect themselves from liability by documenting a well-reasoned course of action that is consistent with ethical principles and that reflects a process involving supervisors and other relevant professionals.

Chapter 1

Ethical Decisionmaking

C hild welfare professionals make decisions on behalf of the state that affect the lives of children and families. Considering all the interests at stake, how do professionals know that their actions are ethical? In making sound decisions, professionals should not rely solely on personal values or intuition, but should incorporate the standards of the profession and current knowledge about the problem with which they are dealing, consult superiors and colleagues, and think critically about the decisions that they must make. When the decision involves an ethical dilemma, professionals should use a model for ethical decisionmaking. The importance of taking these steps in making professional decisions flows from the role of the child welfare professional. As stated in the Illinois *Code of Ethics for Child Welfare Professionals:*

> The child welfare professional is a person who functions in a societally sanctioned decisionmaking capacity for neglected and/or abused children and their families. When individuals accept the role of child welfare professional and the delegated authority inherent in that role, they publicly acknowledge having the professional responsibilities which accompany that authority. Society and agency clients, therefore, have legitimate expectations about the nature of professional intervention as it occurs in one-on-one professional/client interactions, in the management and administration of those providing intervention, and in policy decisionmaking.

To assist child welfare professionals in understanding the nature of ethical decisionmaking, this chapter provides an overview of professional ethics and values and outlines a model for ethical decisionmaking to assist in managing ethical dilemmas. A starting point for ethical decisionmaking is a code of ethics that articulates the values of the profession and sets the guidelines and boundaries of conduct for all within the profession. The Illinois *Code of Ethics for Child Welfare Professionals* and similar codes of ethics for child welfare and other professions describe core values and provide ethical guidance for the profession.

VALUES AND THE FIDUCIARY RELATIONSHIP

There are two concepts that provide a framework for ethical decisionmaking and ethical conduct in providing child welfare services: *values* that underlie ethical child welfare practice and the *fiduciary relationship* that exists between the child welfare professional and the client.

A value is a desirable quality, condition, or practice. When an ethical decision is required, critical thinking is needed about the underlying values and how they should be applied. Values can be described in a variety of ways. Values, for example, may be intrinsic or instrumental. A value is said to be intrinsic if it is desired for its own sake and not for the sake of something further. Examples of intrinsic values are life, security, health, freedom, and self-determination. A value is said to be instrumental if it is desirable as a means to either another instrumental value or an intrinsic value. Wealth, for example, may be considered an instrumental value because it normally is desired as a means to freedom and security. Values also may differ as to whether they are based on principles or standards of right behavior. Values, for example, such as honesty, confidentiality or fairness are expressed as principles or standards of right behavior whereas other values, such as wealth or power, reflect desires that individuals may have as part of a satisfying life, but which do not necessarily relate directly to ethical behavior.

The foundation of the child welfare profession centers around the intrinsic values of protecting children and preserving families. From this foundation, additional values have been identified for respectful intervention with families. As identified in the Illinois *Code of Ethics for Child Welfare Professionals* and generally agreed upon by child welfare professionals, the core child welfare values are:

- Protection of children
- Preservation of families
- Respect for families
- Respect for persons
- Client self-determination
- Individualized intervention
- Competence
- Loyalty
- Diligence
- Honesty
- Promise-keeping
- Confidentiality

In addition to these core child welfare values, agencies with religious affiliations may have certain specific religious principles that affect their child welfare practice.

A fiduciary relationship is a relationship that exists between a professional and a client that is dependent on the client's trust in the professional. As is typically the case in professional-client relationships, the relationship between a child welfare professional and the client is inherently unbalanced because the professional possesses far greater power than the client. Whether the client is voluntary or nonvoluntary, the client must be able to trust that child welfare professionals will use their specialized knowledge and skills in ways that are consistent with professional values. Specifically, clients must be able to trust that child welfare professionals will exercise their authority in the best interest of the child. When child welfare professionals betray the trust that is integral to fiduciary relationships, their unethical conduct affects both clients and the public as a whole.

ETHICAL DECISIONMAKING

In many situations that arise for child welfare professionals, two or more professional values will apply, making it difficult to determine the right course of action. Child welfare professionals must be able to make sound ethical decisions in complicated situations, recognizing that the consequences may not be fully predictable. Ethical decisionmaking is the process of evaluating ethically relevant considerations in choosing a course of action. It is systematic and impartial, having little to do with personal preferences, beliefs, or feelings, and it requires questioning initial feelings, intuitions and biases to discover sound reasons for acting in one way rather than another. Ethical decisionmaking is a skill that can be practiced and improved. This chapter provides a model for ethical decisionmaking that professionals can use to strengthen their skills in this area.

It is important to note that some situations requiring ethical decisionmaking may require a review of relevant literature and research. In addition, when a situation has significant ethical implications for the client, consultation with supervisors and colleagues may be necessary to determine the most appropriate course of action. When situations arise in which a supervisor is uncertain regarding the right course of action, she should seek consultation with the ethics board of the agency or another resource.

An eight-step decisionmaking model may be used to make ethical decisions in complex child welfare matters. To illustrate the use of this model, summarized in Table 1-1, the following case example will be used:

> Maria is the caseworker for Joseph, age 13. Joseph's mother abandoned him when he was seven. Her parental rights were terminated. When he was younger, Joseph often made idealized statements about his mother and expressed longing for her return. In the past three years, Joseph has ceased asking about his mother and now enjoys a good relationship with

Table 1-1. Model for Making Ethical Decisions

① State the problem.

② Check the facts. Does the evidence support the alleged facts?
Have all needed facts been gathered? Which facts are irrelevant?
Have the relevant research and literature been identified?

③ Develop a list of alternative courses of action.

④ Discern what is ethically at stake in relation to each of the alternatives:

   a)   The relevant ethical principles.

   b)   The likely harms and benefits to the parties involved.

   c)   Relevant laws.

   d)   Relevant agency policies.

   e)   Relevant rights and the responsibilities that correspond with those rights.

⑤ Test alternatives.

   Ethical standards test: Does one option fit better with the relevant ethical principles,
   agency policies, and laws than other alternatives?

   Outcomes test: Does one option promise more benefit or less harm than other alternatives?

⑥ Make a decision. Prioritize based on which option is consistent with the most
important values and choose the alternative that maintains the most important values.

⑦ Check the conclusions.

   Publicity test: Would the decision stand if it were to be published in the newspaper?

   Goosey-Gander Test: Would the decision stand if the decisionmaker were adversely
   affected by it? (Is what is good for the goose, good for the gander?)

   Colleague Test: What would colleagues say about the problem and the selected
   option? Would colleagues raise any problem with the selected option?

   Professional Test: What might the profession's governing body or ethics committee
   say about the option? Would their response be sound?

   Organizational Test: What would the agency's ethics officer or legal counsel say about
   the selected option? Would that response be sound?

⑧ Plan for prevention of the problem in the future.

   What would make it less likely that such a decision must be made again? Are there
   steps that could be taken at the professional level to avoid the problem in the future?
   Are there steps that could be taken at the organizational level to avoid the problem in
   the future?

(Ozar & Sokol 1994; Davis 1997; Gambrill & Gibbs 2002)

his current foster parents, who are in the process of adopting him. Maria was recently informed of the death of Joseph's birthmother and struggles with the decision of whether or not to tell Joseph.

Step 1: State the problem.

The first step in ethical decisionmaking is to state the problem clearly. The key to defining an ethical problem is to identify two or more ethically important considerations that are in conflict. When the problem is specified in this manner, initial ethical worries may prove unwarranted, or the ethical problem may be quite different from what it initially appeared to be. In the case example, the problem might be stated as the competing values of Maria's obligation to be truthful with Joseph (and/or Joseph's right to know of his mother's death) and Maria's responsibility to refrain from harming Joseph.

Step 2: Check the facts.

Ethical decisionmaking requires that the child welfare professional work with facts and not with unwarranted assumptions or suppositions. Facts must be determined and verified to ensure that the correct values are prioritized and that important relevant values are not overlooked. When the child welfare professional confirms the facts of a case, she can clarify any unwarranted assumptions that may have been made, identify any additional information that is needed, and identify and set aside irrelevant information. In the case example, if Joseph's mother's death were a rumor that Maria heard from someone in the neighborhood where he formerly lived, she should not consider telling Joseph until she verifies that the death occurred.

Checking the facts should clarify the following: Joseph's mother has died; Joseph does not know that his mother has died; Joseph has a good relationship with his foster parents; and information about Joseph's mother caused him pain in the past.

Step 3: Develop a list of alternative courses of action.

The next step is to develop a list of all possible courses of action. For example, in the case study, Maria could:
- Not tell Joseph.
- Tell Joseph plainly.
- Decide to tell Joseph only if he asks.
- Not tell Joseph even if he asks.
- Inform Joseph's foster parents and have them tell Joseph.

There may be additional options which Maria will add as she proceeds with the decisionmaking process.

Step 4: Identify what is ethically at stake in each alternative.

Making good ethical decisions requires the ability to recognize what is ethically at stake in any given situation. As assessment of what is ethically at stake requires an understanding of:

- The professional's own personal values

- Relevant ethical principles of the profession

- Current information in the field

- Relevant laws, regulations, and agency policies

- Relevant rights and corresponding responsibilities and the individuals who have these rights and responsibilities

- Current data and research in the field that further inform the above

In the case example, Maria should consult the code of ethics for her agency and any laws, rules, or agency policies bearing on such disclosures to children in care. She should be aware of how her own personal ethical code may affect her view of the situation and not let it override professional values. She may find, as is the case in the Illinois *Code of Ethics for Child Welfare Professionals*, that those professional values include honesty and the duty to minimize harm to a client. Applying these values, she may wonder whether she would be dishonest if she were to choose not to inform Joseph about his mother's death. She may also wonder whether telling him or not telling him will cause him unwarranted emotional harm, both in the short term and in the long term. She will realize that she faces a possible conflict between the two values of honesty and minimizing harm. With regard to rights and responsibilities, she may intuitively feel that Joseph has a right to know about his mother, but she may not be sure whether her corresponding responsibility is to proactively inform him or just truthfully answer if he asks. She must also sort out her responsibilities toward the foster parents. For example, she may have an ethical responsibility to be honest and cooperative with them but a legal responsibility to retain decisionmaking authority in the case.

Finally, Maria should consult current research to learn whether any studies have addressed the emotional impact of revelations of a parent's death on a child of Joseph's age and experience. There might also be research on the opposite side of this question:

Can long-term emotional harm result from a child's later realization that important facts about his identity were concealed from him? Using knowledge in this way is called evidence-based practice, "the conscientious, explicit, and judicious use of current best evidence in making decisions about the care of individuals" (Sactrett, Richardson, & Haynes, 1997).

Step 5: Test alternatives.

There are two general approaches to testing alternatives through a process of ethical decisionmaking: the ethical standards test and the outcomes test. The ethical standards test holds that certain actions are inherently ethical or unethical, and the outcomes test holds that actions are ethical or unethical depending on whether they result in beneficial or harmful outcomes to those involved. Professionals may have a preference for one test over another but should use both tests when making ethical decisions.

The Ethical Standards Test

The ethical standards test evaluates ethical rightness by appealing to a set of ethical standards and values. This approach (called "deontological" by ethicists) holds that certain actions are inherently unethical because they treat persons as objects; violate agreements or promises; or are irrational in some way. When faced with an ethical decision, the child welfare professional should first consult an ethical code or other ethical resource in order to choose the course of action that best conforms with the relevant ethical standards. This method of ethical decisionmaking is relatively straightforward: the child welfare professional selects the course of action that best fits with articulated ethical standards.

Some ethical standards, such as avoiding conflicts of interest, are made explicit in professional codes. Other ethical standards, such as "do not lie," may be both codified as ethical standards for a profession and exist as unwritten social standards. In either case, ethical standards express values.

The ethical standards approach commonly refers to rights. A right is an entitlement that creates corresponding responsibility for others, to act in a certain way or to refrain from interfering with the individual who holds the right. Recognition of rights increases the likelihood that individuals treat one another in an acceptable way. Rights may be classified in a number of ways:

> **Positive or Negative.** A right is positive if it requires others to take affirmative action in a certain way or to meet a certain need. For example, a child has a positive right to a safe and secure environment.

Parents, the child's caregiver, or the state must exert effort to ensure the child's safety and security. A right is negative if it requires that others refrain from interfering. For example, a parent's right to raise his or her child as he or she sees fit requires that others not interfere.

Universal or Particular. Everyone is entitled to a universal right. An example is the right of each person to food or shelter. A right is particular if it only applies to certain individuals in specific situations. A particular right is a client's right to confidentiality in a professional relationship.

Absolute or Qualified. A right is absolute if it cannot be taken away or overridden, such as a child's right to be protected from abuse. A right is qualified if the right can be overridden. Parents have the right to care for their children as they see fit only to the extent that they protect their children from harm.

To reason effectively with regard to rights, it is important to identify a right as positive or negative, universal or particular, and absolute or qualified. For example, a parent has a right to raise her own child, but her right is qualified and may be overridden by the child's absolute right to be raised in a safe environment. When a conflict develops between the parent's right to parent and the child's right to safety, the absolute right will prevail over the qualified right. The nature and extent of any responsibility will depend on the nature of the right to which it corresponds. A positive right generates the responsibility to take proactive steps in response to that right, whereas a negative right is associated with the responsibility to refrain from interfering.

Applying the ethical standards test to the case example, the following might take place:

Maria consults the agency's code of ethics. When she finds that it requires honesty with clients, she believes that Joseph has a right to know, which implies that she would have a responsibility to tell him of his mother's death. She concludes that it would be unethical to withhold such information from Joseph. She is aware that Joseph may possibly experience emotional distress, but nevertheless, she tells him of his mother's death.

Many child welfare professionals would make the same decision as Maria. It is important, however, to consider the limitations of this test:

First, when using this approach, it may be difficult to resolve conflicts among standards. In the case example, Maria has both the responsibility to be honest with Joseph and also not to harm him. She may believe, based on her second responsibility, that informing Joseph of his mother's death would harm him. Which ethical standard—honesty or the duty not to harm—is more important?

Second, it may be difficult to apply general ethical standards to specific situations. Codes of ethics, by nature, are general. Any attempt to anticipate a myriad of specific ethical dilemmas would lead to several thick volumes of text, and even in such a case, the exact situation that must be addressed may not be covered. Consequently, a set of ethical standards may not be as helpful as a professional would hope in giving clear guidance on day-to-day situations.

Third, framing ethical issues in terms of rights is only a starting point. To have a right to act in a certain way means only that it is permissible to act that way. The question remains whether one may ethically do so. For example, an adoptive parent may have a right to prohibit any contact between his adopted child and the child's birthparents. Nevertheless, depending on the circumstances, the child's best interest may mean that birthparents be allowed to participate in the child's life, and allowing contact may be ethically advisable.

Fourth, merely stating that a right exists does nothing to clarify the extent of an individual's responsibility. Further, stating the existence of a right is not helpful in identifying who, in particular, has the responsibility. Determining that Joseph has a right to know, for example, does not clarify who would have the responsibility to tell him about his mother's death.

Fifth, the reference to rights can obscure what, in reality, is ethically at stake in a situation because individuals often claim rights without a clear basis for their claim. A foster parent, for example, may claim the right to prohibit visits between a child and the child's biological parent because of concerns about the impact of visits on the child. When they are not carefully considered, claims to rights may get in the way of clear ethical discussion.

The Outcomes Test

A second test in ethical decisionmaking is the outcomes test. Although this test acknowledges the usefulness of the ethical standards test, the outcomes test evaluates ethical rightness on the level of benefit that an action produces as opposed to other alternatives. Under this approach, an ethical action is that action, among all available alternatives, that produces the most favorable balance of benefit over harm to all those involved. Benefit primarily refers to the promotion of such intrinsic values as physical and emotional health, security, fulfillment, and freedom. Harm refers to the diminution of those values. When applying the outcomes test, both short-term and long-term consequences must be considered. For example, misleading a client may provide certain short-term benefits to the client, but in the long run, it may harm the client in significant ways as well as undermine the professional relationship.

The decisionmaking process involved in the outcomes test consists of developing alternative courses of action and selecting the one that maximizes benefit and minimizes harm for all of the involved individuals both in the short and long term. The outcomes test necessarily requires prioritization of alternative courses of action based on outcomes. Prioritization of options takes into account three main factors: the degree of potential harm and benefit, the likelihood that harm and/or benefit will occur, and the number of persons affected.

If Maria used the outcomes test to reach her decision, the following might occur:

> Maria considers the consequences of informing Joseph of his mother's death. She predicts that it would cause him emotional distress, and given his traumatic experience with abandonment, she believes that the news may cause him to act out. Because he is now doing very well in his preadoptive home and not talking about his mother, she believes that he may benefit from not knowing. Maria feels that the potential harm outweighs any benefits of informing Joseph. She decides not to tell him unless he asks about his mother.

Although Maria decided not to tell Joseph because she thought that doing so would likely cause more harm than benefit, others might disagree. Another person might balance the harm and benefit differently, concluding that withholding the information, in the long run, may result in more harm than benefit. It is important to note that different ethical tests do not automatically lead to different conclusions and that the ethical standards and outcomes tests will often suggest the same course of action. Use of both approaches together, however, is key to making effective, organized ethical decisions.

Like the ethical standards test, the outcomes test has limitations. First, outcomes may be difficult to predict. Maria, for example, assumes that Joseph would be upset and act impulsively if he discovered his mother has died, but his reaction may be quite different.

Second, the focus of the outcomes approach may not give sufficient attention to other significant ethical considerations. For instance, the outcomes approach conceivably could be used to justify lying to maximize benefit or minimize harm. Maria, for example, might decide to mislead Joseph about his mother even if he asks to minimize the possibility of emotional distress.

Third, the outcomes approach might cause the child welfare professional to overlook relational duties. When there is a personal or professional relationship, certain obligations arise to the other party that do not exist as to others. A child welfare professional, for example, has special obligations to her client that she does not have to non-clients. Acting in accordance with these responsibilities may or may not maximize benefit in a given situation, but, nevertheless, will be ethically required. In the case study, for example, Joseph's foster parents might urge Maria not to inform him of his mother's death. Maria might reason, on the basis of their wishes, that withholding the information would maximize benefit for Joseph and his foster parents (or minimize harm to them). Nonetheless, because Maria's primary responsibility is to Joseph, she must base her decision on her duties to Joseph and not upon the desires of his foster parents.

Fourth, the outcomes approach has historically been criticized for promoting the benefit of the majority while marginalizing the minority. In situations in which one cannot maximize benefit for everyone, an outcomes approach may recommend maximizing benefit for as many people as possible. As a consequence, individuals who are not among the majority will not enjoy the benefit. Questions about fairness or justice are raised when decisions yield such outcomes.

Because of the limitations of both approaches, it is best to integrate both into the ethical reasoning and decisionmaking process. The approaches reflect two levels of ethical reasoning, with the first level appealing to ethical standards. In the many cases in which standards conflict or are too general to be helpful, it becomes important to consider the possible outcomes of different courses of action. In such situations, the course of action that promises the most favorable balance of benefit over harm (both short-term and long-term) is usually, though not always, the better alternative.

Step 6: Make a choice.

Once the ethical standards test and the outcomes test have been conducted, a choice must be made. In many instances, conflicts will occur between important values and it will not be possible to pursue an alternative that preserves all of the relevant values. Prioritizing alternatives involves prioritizing ethical standards and outcomes.

Prioritizing ethical standards and outcomes is the most difficult part of the decision-making process. The following are guidelines for this process:

1. Ethical standards and outcomes that prevent basic harms (such as death, serious physical injury, or lack of food or shelter) should be a first consideration in prioritizing ethical concerns (Reamer, 1990). As an example, the removal of children from their parents' custody is justified when there is a risk of physical harm to

them because the prevention of serious harm overrides the parents' right to keep their children in their home.

It sometimes happens that allowing a client to exercise her individual freedom (self-determination) could harm others. As an example, the value of confidentiality may be overridden when maintaining confidentiality would place at risk the life or physical well-being of others. If a parent reveals to a counselor that she abuses her children, the counselor must report this even though it was shared in confidence. The duty to report is even stronger because of the counselor's commitment to abide by ethical standards of his or her profession. In such cases, professionals forfeit the right to act in ways that may be permissible for others. Mental health and child welfare professionals, for example, are obligated to report any suspected instances of child abuse or neglect, whereas members of the general public are encouraged but are not ethically required to do so. Another example of professional conduct that would be ethically justifiable based on the prevention of basic harms is in the domestic violence arena. A professional might deny knowing the whereabouts of a woman fleeing domestic violence if he is confronted by her abuser. A lie may be ethically acceptable because it protects the life or physical well-being of another.

2. Although it is generally true that a risk of basic harm should take priority over all other ethical considerations, a risk of basic harm may be overridden by an individual's right to freedom (or self-determination) when the harm threatened is only to himself (Reamer, 1990). A 15-year-old, for example, may decide that he does not want to be adopted and may refuse an opportunity to meet a prospective adoptive family. Although others may feel that adoption is in his best interests, he has the right to self-determination (as discussed more fully in Chapter 3).

It is important to note that in some cases, a self-determined decision that brings harm to the individual herself may also harm those who depend on her. For example, a mother may decide to remain in an abusive situation and her children may suffer emotional harm when they witness the ongoing abuse.

How should Maria make her choice about telling Joseph? She needs to weigh the importance and practical consequences of the two ethical principles at stake here: honesty and minimizing harm. If there were little harm that could be predicted from telling Joseph, honesty would be the best course. Predicting harm to Joseph may be complicated, however. How prepared is Joseph to process this information? What would be the emotional impact on him both now and into the future from telling or not telling him? How important is it to his sense of personal identity to know about his birthmother? Could the adoption process be derailed if he were told? To determine these things, Maria should pay close attention to Joseph's behaviors and statements. She should consult with his foster parents and therapist, if any, and look back through his case file for clues to how he might react. She should check research in the field to see if there are relevant studies about the psychological reactions of abused children to the death of a birthparent, or on the necessity of emotional ties to the birthfamily as an element of personal identity. Finally, she should weigh all the benefits of telling that she has identified against the predicted negative consequences in Joseph's case and choose the weightier side of the scale. As should be apparent, the right option will be heavily dependent on the specific facts in Joseph's case.

Step 7: Check conclusions.

Once Maria has reached a tentative conclusion, she should discuss it with her supervisor before executing her decision. By nature, ethical dilemmas tend to be complex and require educated judgment calls. A caseworker should always think through the problem with a supervisor unless it is impossible because of time constraints. If her agency has an ethics committee, the professional could also ask the committee's advice.

The professional might also consider what others would say; how she herself would react if she were among those negatively affected by the decision; or how other colleagues would respond. If these reactions would be negative, it is important to isolate the reasons. Is there something that has been missed or ignored in the analysis? These methods of checking conclusions, however, are not as important as the professional's reasoning through the ethical standards or outcomes test. Although the reactions of others can assist in identifying errors in reasoning, it is also important to recognize that colleagues will not always support a professional's decision. At the same time, the ethical decisionmaking process should not be used in isolation, but in conjunction with colleagues, particularly supervisors.

Because Joseph's mother has already passed away, Maria can take some time to make her decision and check her conclusions. She can consult with her supervisor, ethics committee, and other professionals about her ethical reasoning process. If the situation were more of an emergency (for example, if Joseph's mother were dying and requested to see him), Maria might only have time to consult with her supervisor. Since there are rarely answers in ethics that do not involve unavoidable harms, the more consultation Maria seeks, the more comfortable she should feel that her solution maximizes benefits and minimizes harms to Joseph.

Step 8: Avoid similar dilemmas in the future.

After the professional has made and checked her decision, the next step is to ask if this situation could have been avoided, and if so, how. Future dilemmas can sometimes be avoided through a careful assessment of the level of support received from supervisors and colleagues in the decisionmaking process. Thought should be given regarding others who should be consulted if a similar dilemma arises in the future. Finally, consideration should be given to whether the ethical problem was caused by organizational factors. Would a rule or policy change have prevented the problem? If so, what can be done to change organizational factors that contributed to the situation?

Could Maria's dilemma have been avoided or minimized? Are there contributing factors that could be addressed so that similar problems do not occur in the future? Some ethical dilemmas are inevitable, and this may be one of them. If, for example, Maria knew in advance that Joseph's mother was terminally ill, she might have had more time to think through the problem or broaden her options. Perhaps giving Joseph a chance to say goodbye to his mother or asking her to leave some memento which could be given to Joseph would produce a better outcome for the child. In general, the death of a birthparent of a child in foster care is not an unusual occurrence; Maria's agency might consider providing caseworkers with an outline of the right questions to ask and options to consider in such a situation.

SUMMARY

Child welfare professionals should be familiar with and turn to the existing codes of ethics when making decisions that have ethical consequences. As an example, the Illinois *Code of Ethics for Child Welfare Professionals* articulates the values of the profession and principles necessary for working within fiduciary relationships. Codes of ethics, however, do not offer pat solutions for every ethical dilemma that can occur in child welfare, and professionals may have to make difficult choices that require sacrificing one ethical value to maintain another. Child welfare professionals should consider ethical decisionmaking a necessary skill they can always improve. Ethical decisionmaking should not be done in isolation but in collaboration with supervisors, administrators, and ethics boards. The eight steps of the decisionmaking model outlined in Table 1-1 can assist with most ethical dilemmas.

CASE STUDIES FOR CHAPTER 1

Case Study 1-1. Lindy, a child welfare caseworker, makes quick decisions about his clients based on his first impression of them. Most of his clients, according to Lindy, are "immoral" because they have had children out of wedlock, are living "in sin," or are addicted to drugs. He feels that because of their "corrupting" influence on children, these parents do not deserve to have their children returned to them. What effect will Lindy's attitudes likely have on his casework?

Case Study 1-2. Tasha, a client whose children are currently in foster care, loves her children. On several occasions, she has been come very close to having them returned home. On each of the three occasions when her children were about to be returned home, however, she has done something to "sabotage" their return. Her caseworker has begun to wonder if Tasha wants her children returned to her. Is there a third option that her caseworker can offer other than returning her children to her or terminating parental rights?

Case Study 1-3. For the first time, Jennifer is working with a client, Sue, who is said to have a mental illness. Jennifer intuitively thinks that there may be special considerations that apply to her work with Sue. What issues should she anticipate? What resources should she use? Should she consult with others?

Case Study 1-4. Jared, a foster care caseworker, cannot decide if he should recommend a change in the permanency goal for Shari (a 13-year old) from adoption to independence. What are the likely benefits and harms he must consider?

Case Study 1-5. Delera likes her client Patty very much. Because Patty knows that Delera drives past her home when she leaves work, Patty asks Delera for a ride. Delera's first reaction is to take Patty home because she knows that this help will make it easier for Patty to get to her night job on time. Delera then remembers that her coworkers never drive their clients home. What should Delera do?

Case Study 1-6. Clark decides not to recommend to the court that Debbie's children return home because Debbie did not attend mandated parenting classes. The court, however, continues the case after determining that Debbie could not have attended parenting classes because she did not have transportation and could not arrange child care for the two children at home with her. What should Clark be thinking about for future cases?

Chapter 2

Integrity

C hild welfare professionals are expected to demonstrate integrity in their inter-
actions with clients and to promote integrity within their agencies. Integrity
means more than simply acting ethically. Persons who have integrity understand their professional values, are committed to them, and practice those professional values. Their conduct is ultimately consistent with their professed values. Child welfare professionals who have integrity deliver superior services and also promote
integrity throughout their agencies. This chapter defines integrity and examines how
integrity can be hindered or enabled in child welfare agencies.

WHAT IS INTEGRITY?

Integrity can be defined as a characteristic of individuals who integrate their values into
their character and make ethical choices as a result. "Integrity" arises from the same
root as the word "integrate." Individuals who possess integrity are, in a sense, "integrated": their professional values inform their character and their character shapes their
conduct. Integrity requires three components: knowledge of the right values, the right
motive (character), and doing the right thing (conduct). Unless all of the components
are present, an individual cannot be said have integrity.

As discussed in Chapter 1, the core values of child welfare professionals include: protection of children, preservation of families, respect for persons, client self-determination, individualized intervention, competence, loyalty, honesty, promise-keeping, and
confidentiality. In the context of integrity, these values are an integral part of the decisions that child welfare professionals make. Although integrity begins with a knowledge of what is important (values), it also requires acting on that knowledge.

Character is the desire and willingness to practice in accordance with professed values.
Simple good-heartedness, by itself, does not constitute integrity. Self-interest (fear of
being fired, for example) and expediency similarly do not constitute integrity, even if
the individual's resulting conduct is consistent with his responsibilities and obligations.
An individual must be able to translate values into the right courses of action in order
to have integrity. The conduct of a person with integrity is based on values, a commitment to acting on those values, and his responsibilities and obligations.

In an effort to maintain ethical behavior, many agencies try to enforce stringent rules to motivate and maintain right conduct. Although rules and policies are important to agency operations, this strategy requires very close monitoring of employees' conduct. It also means that goals are limited to staying within the bounds of minimal expectations.

When an agency has employees with integrity, it need not use its resources to monitor and enforce rules and regulations. When professionals understand and accept professional values and those values shape their character, they desire to act and, in fact, do act in accordance with their values. Internal, not external, factors cause them to act ethically. When employees adopt the values of the organization, they personally share in its successes and strive to avoid failures. They make efforts by spending more time and energy pursuing and becoming connected to the organization's mission. The following example compares a child welfare professional who has integrity with one who merely follows rules and regulations.

> Betty and Izumi have similar clients. Both clients are 7-year-old boys who have been sexually abused. Betty and Izumi both do assessments and discover that the boys are suffering from depression and are having behavior problems. Betty and Izumi both complete the necessary paperwork to obtain counseling services. Three weeks later, neither has heard if her request has been approved.

> Betty does not worry. She has followed the rules and regulations of her agency and met her obligation by filing the request for service.

> Izumi has become worried about her client. The client has become more and more depressed, and Izumi realizes that he is in dire need of special services. Because Izumi wants her client to be served, she calls the office where she filed her request. She is told that they are very busy and will not be able to review her request for another two weeks. Izumi argues in vain that her client's need is immediate. She goes to her supervisor and explains the situation. Her supervisor calls the special services office and tells the worker that if the request is not processed immediately, he will contact her supervisor. Izumi's request is processed the next day, and her client receives services the next week.

Note that although Betty may have understood the values of the child welfare profession, her character has not been formed by these values. Her motivation is only to do her job within the regulations set by her agency. Although her actions might be ethically defensible in that she followed organizational procedures, she did not reflect on the detriment to her client should services be delayed for an extended period of time.

In contrast, Izumi's character appears shaped by the values of the child welfare profession. She is primarily concerned that her client receive the services that he needs. She takes additional steps and invests considerably more time serving her client than the organization procedures require. As a result, her client receives the service.

Persons with integrity must have reflective ability, that is, the ability to identify the values at stake among the alternative courses of action and determine which choice best maintains the most important professional values. This task is not simple because, in any given situation, it is likely that values will conflict. As discussed in Chapter 1, such conflicts require prioritization so that the most important values are preserved. An individual of integrity must recognize value-related issues when they arise and reason through them to ensure that choices are supported by relevant values. Reflective ability makes it possible to connect the components of values, character, and conduct. Integrity, however, may not simply be a matter of choice for each individual professional. Employees are influenced by the work environment, which may hinder or support integrity.

INTEGRITY IN THE INDIVIDUAL AND THE ORGANIZATION

Just as an individual may possess or lack integrity, so too may an organization. Child welfare agencies, like individuals, manifest certain values. An agency may be said to lack integrity if its policies and actions do not resonate with the values articulated in its mission statement. The integrity of the organization affects the professionals who work there and, in turn, the services delivered to clients.

A number of organizational factors can prevent professionals from acting with integrity in their service delivery. The most common threats to integrity (and, in fact, to ethics in general) relate to everyday pressures and influences. These pressures range from budgetary constraints and quota expectations to miscommunication and poor relationships with coworkers. As an example, if a caseworker feels she cannot talk to her supervisor, she may not tell her that a newly assigned case does not, as she was originally told, involve one child but a family of five children. Similarly, a professional may not fully respond to a client's needs because of significant pressures from administration to close cases. The following case provides an example of organizational barriers to integrity:

> Juanita is a caseworker. Recently, several caseworkers left her agency. As a result, she is currently carrying 40 cases. Because she is overwhelmed with work, she has made assumptions about what her clients will need as she has developed case plans for 10 of her cases, rather than doing detailed assessments of the families.

In this case, Juanita is attempting to do her best, but the size of her caseload is too large to allow her to properly serve her clients. Consequently, she cuts corners and sacrifices the ethical values of individualized service and competence. Environmental conditions such as excessive caseloads and high staff turnover are key factors that can hinder the integrity of individual employees.

As common sense suggests, it is much easier to integrate values into character and conduct when values and standards of conduct are woven into the fabric of the daily operations of the work environment. It is very difficult for a person of integrity to ethically survive in an organization that itself lacks integrity. Most individuals cannot maintain a high level of professional integrity when the work environment does not reinforce and sustain integrity. At the same time, it is easier for individuals to maintain integrity when they work in an environment which itself has integrity. It is difficult for an individual to remain uncommitted in an environment of ethically committed professionals.

Integrity is promoted when the work environment supports professionals and ensures reasonable workloads, sufficient resources, and feasible deadlines. Even when the work environment is not fully supportive of professionals' integrity, they may be able to develop courses of action that are consistent with integrity. The following alternative version of Juanita's decisionmaking illustrates such a course of action:

> Juanita is a caseworker. Recently several caseworkers left her agency. As a result, she is currently carrying a caseload of 40 cases. Because she is overloaded with work, she prioritizes her workload after discussing this approach with her supervisor. She gives full services to families whose children recently entered foster care and who have the greatest chance of having their children returned home. She provides minimum services to families whose children have been in foster care for many years and have made little progress. She writes a memorandum for each of the cases for which she has minimized services, explaining her reasoning.

Juanita utilizes a triage approach, that is, she assigns priority to projects on the basis of where services, funds, and resources could be best used or were most needed. She uses her time and resources in the most productive way, and she is able to justify her lack of fully comprehensive services to less responsive families by explaining time constraints and the need to provide service to families with more promising outcomes. This reasoning will provide a solid explanation should her services to any of these families be questioned. Her approach is consistent with documentation guidelines for purposes of legal protection: making decisions with others, such as one's supervisor; recording the professionals consulted in making the decision; recording the reasoning behind the decision; and noting any research that supports the decision.

Individuals can greatly influence the conduct and character of others. When individuals have opportunities to observe others who have been able to integrate certain values into their character and conduct, they can develop higher levels of professional integrity. For administrators and supervisors, these realities are noteworthy because they suggest the importance of role-modeling. When individuals in authority model values, those values are more likely to be embraced throughout the organization.

SUMMARY

Integrity means that one's personal and professional values are consistently integrated with character and conduct. Ethical behavior is more likely because it is driven by the professional's internally motivated commitment to ethical conduct. Barriers to integrity tend to be the mundane pressures of organizational life. Agencies can foster integrity among staff by providing a reasonable workload and sufficient resources, encouraging a supportive atmosphere among peers, and providing good role modeling.

CASE STUDIES FOR CHAPTER 2

Case Study 2-1. Lipa has been working at the Gamma Agency for three months. She loves children and makes extra efforts to ensure her clients receive all the services they need. At Gamma, several child welfare workers provide their clients with only the minimal level of services that they must provide. They seldom express concern for their clients. Lipa has seen some caseworkers make case notes about visiting clients whom they have not visited. Some caseworkers are attempting to discourage Lipa from making extra efforts. She is beginning to feel depressed and is starting to dread work. What should Lipa do?

Case Study 2-2. Jessica is very kind to her clients. She regularly promises to help them; offers extra visits with their children; tells them that she will inquire about additional benefits for which they may be eligible; and promises to advocate for them in court. Frequently, however, Jessica does not follow through on these promises. Does Jessica have integrity?

Case Study 2-3. Albert is the caseworker for Ruby and her 8-year-old son, Rod. Ruby is in prison. Ruby does not want Rod to visit her because she does not want him to see her in prison nor does she want him exposed to that environment. Albert has promised to carry messages from Ruby to Rod. As Ruby was preparing for her parole hearing, she begged Albert to tell Rod that she would be released soon. Albert, however, knows that Ruby's chances of being paroled are slim. What should he do? How should Albert use reflective ability?

Chapter 3

Client Self-Determination
and Informed Consent

Most people prefer to make their own decisions and resent being excluded when decisions that affect their lives are being made. Decisions that affect an individual's private or family life are particularly sensitive. When clients become involved involuntarily with the child welfare system, there is little room for them to make many of their own decisions or to be self-determining. They find themselves in the unenviable situation of having their family life exposed and scrutinized by social workers and the court while, at the same time, being subjected to substantial requirements to make changes in their lives.

The role of the child welfare professional is to fully inform clients about the situation they face as a result of their involvement with the child welfare system; assess the client's decisionmaking capacities; and provide the client with opportunities to participate in the more flexible aspects of his or her service plan. This practice respects the rights of the client and is a first step toward helping the client regain control of his or her life.

This chapter defines self-determination in relation to clients who become involuntarily involved with the child welfare system (mandated clients), discusses how to respect and promote client self-determination, and describes situations when it may be necessary to override a client's decision or preference. It concludes with a discussion of informed consent.

SELF-DETERMINATION IN CHILD WELFARE

Self-determination is the capacity of an individual to determine the course of his or her life through the choices that he or she makes. This capacity enables individuals to exercise freedom. Indeed, the capacity to be self-determining is one of the core features of being a person.

Treating clients properly requires respecting, to the fullest extent possible, their self-determination. The value of respecting and promoting self-determination is fundamental to the helping professions. In fact, when individuals seek the help of professionals, it is because they have lost control over some aspect of their lives and wish to regain it. Although most child welfare clients do not freely seek out the assistance of the child welfare system, they do choose to maintain a relationship with child welfare professionals to regain control over those aspects of their lives that involve their children. As a result, key goals of the work that child welfare professionals undertake with their clients include helping them regain control over their lives and promoting their self-determination.

In some professions, respecting client self-determination simply means respect for the client's decisions, whatever they may be. Parents who become child welfare clients, however, have limited options. They do not freely seek out the assistance of child welfare agencies but rather are forced to become clients because the state has reason to believe that they have been abusive or neglectful to their children. As a result, there are legitimate nonnegotiable constraints on their self-determination. If they are to regain custody of their children, they must comply with requirements set by the state. For example, parents may be required to submit to routine drug screening, participate in a substance abuse treatment program, attend therapy, or enroll in parenting classes. Child welfare clients do not have the freedom of choice that clients normally have when they seek professional assistance.

They do, however, continue to have a right of self-determination in two important ways: the right to make the choices available to them without undue influence or coercion and the right to receive the information they need to make a self-determined choice. At the same time, there are opportunities to respect and promote client self-determination, and child welfare professionals are obligated to identify and act on those opportunities.

RESPECTING AND PROMOTING CLIENT SELF-DETERMINATION

Enabling mandated clients to be self-determining within the constraints of the child welfare system is both an ethical and a practical course of action. Promoting client self-determination recognizes the rights of clients and is a step toward assisting clients to take control of their own lives. When clients are involved in shaping the service plan, they tend to have greater ownership and greater commitment to achieving its goals.

The most obvious way to promote client self-determination is to identify decisions that clients can make and give them options from which to choose. Decisionmaking capability is task-specific, that is, competence is relative to the specific task under consideration. Although a client is restricted from or incapable of making decisions about one aspect of her life, she may be quite capable of making decisions about other aspects of her life. The extent of her ability to make decisions will depend upon the type of decision that must be made. For example, a young child may not be capable of choosing who should be responsible for her care, but she may be quite capable of choosing whether visits with her parents should take place at a playground or a restaurant. The key is to identify which decisions are within the capacity of clients to make and which are not. In addition, it is important to identify and counteract the factors that may limit client's self-determination.

IDENTIFYING AND ADDRESSING FACTORS THAT LIMIT SELF-DETERMINATION

The child welfare professional should explain to the client at the outset of the relationship which decisions she can make and which decisions are beyond her control. This discussion should take into account the common limits on a client's decision-making capacity. The child welfare professional should be aware of ways to compensate for these factors in the delivery of services so that the client can be as self-determining as each situation permits.

The Factors that Limit Self-Determination

Lack of information, false information, or false beliefs. Clients cannot make good decisions if they are not adequately informed or are making decisions based upon false beliefs. One obvious way to address this limit to self-determination is to keep the client fully informed so that when there is an opportunity to express a preference or make a choice, the client's preference or choice is based upon sufficient information. The client also must be clearly informed of the probable consequences of each decision that she is entitled to make. When the client makes a choice, the child welfare professional should encourage her to explain her rationale so that the professional can determine if she has made any false assumptions or has misunderstood certain information. This process requires a commitment of sufficient time to ensure that the client has the information she needs and that it is presented in a way that she can best understand.

Diminished cognitive capacity. Cognitive capacity is the ability to receive, process, and assimilate information. A client's cognitive capacity may interfere with his or her ability to understand and process information. Cognitive capacity may be hampered by age, developmental disability, substance abuse, or other factors. When it is suspected that a client's cognitive capacity is impaired, psychological testing should be considered to provide a better understanding of the client's decisionmaking ability. Because psychological assessments can take time and are not appropriate in every case, however, the child welfare professional may have to make judgments about the client's abilities. If the client appears to have a cognitive deficit, the professional should make every attempt to improve the client's decisionmaking capacity by informing him of his circumstances and options in a way that he can understand. In some cases, however, it may be necessary to work with relatives, significant others, or the client's lawyer to ensure that the client understands his situation. In other cases, it may be necessary for the child welfare professional or another person to make decisions on behalf of the client.

The complexity of the child welfare system. Even when clients have normal cognitive capacities, the complexity of the child welfare system can be confusing and overwhelming. Child welfare professionals must make every effort to ensure that clients have an adequate understanding of the child welfare system so that they can make educated choices. At the same time, when a client is confused and overwhelmed, she is likely to become fearful and anxious. These feelings are likely to diminish the client's ability to think clearly. The child welfare professional should avoid holding important discussions in atmospheres that are likely to cause or heighten the client's fear or anxiety.

Language difficulties. It is not uncommon to encounter language-related difficulties with clients. Some clients are not native speakers of the English language. A child welfare professional may need to transfer a case to a professional with foreign-language speaking ability. At the very least, if the client cannot speak English and the child welfare professional does not speak the client's language, an interpreter must be provided for the client. Even when a client is a native English speaker, she may not be able to understand the information that is being provided because of the technical terminology of the child welfare system. When clients cannot decipher what is being said, they cannot adequately understand their situation or make self-determined judgments. Child welfare professionals should avoid needless technical jargon when they speak with clients.

Mental illness. Mental illness can have a significant impact on decisionmaking ability as well as overall behavior. If it appears that a client is mentally ill, the child welfare professional may need a psychological consultation to better understand the client's capabilities. Whenever possible, significant decisions should be postponed until the client's mental illness can be addressed. At the same time, however, delays in decisionmaking may have a detrimental effect on children and should be carefully evaluated.

Reaction to the mandated situation. Because the mandated situation is an intrusion into the client's life, clients may react to the loss of freedom with behaviors based in fear, anxiety, anger, or denial. These reactions may interfere with the client's judgment.

The client's behavior may be offensive or appear uncooperative, giving the child welfare professional a highly negative first impression of the client. This behavior must be understood as a response to the situation and not necessarily indicative of who the client is as a person. It is important that child welfare professionals recognize and cope with these behaviors in a way that builds rapport with clients and assists them to function in the most self-determined manner possible (Rooney, 1992).

Psychosocial factors. Psychosocial factors are elements of the individual's development, personal history, or present environment that influence his or her behavior. The behavior of teenagers well illustrates the impact of psychosocial factors on behavior. Young adolescents are struggling with their identity and may "try out" certain behaviors and then abandon them; some adolescents may be resistant to authority because they are establishing their independence; and adolescents, because they are concerned about what their peers think, may make decisions depending upon what they believe will be perceived as "cool" to their friends. In the professional situation, a client may be influenced in her decisionmaking and express preferences that are not fully her own. For example, a woman in a violent relationship may make decisions based on maintaining safety. An abusive partner may be controlling the client in such a way that she does not feel safe to make the decisions that she really wants to make. These psychosocial factors may have a significant impact on the client's ability to exercise the right of self-determination.

Addressing the Factors that Limit Self-Determination

Respecting and promoting the self-determination of clients when there are limitations requires much more than simply allowing the client to make choices. The child welfare professional must make every effort to offset the factors that may inhibit self-determination. First, the professional should evaluate the decisionmaking capacity of the client and reevaluate it appropriately as circumstances change. This evaluation process involves an assessment of the client' decisionmaking ability based on the following questions:

1. Is the decision or preference consistent with the client's values? Is the client making a decision or expressing a preference that is inconsistent with preferences she has expressed throughout the professional relationship?

   If, for example, a client has been working to regain custody of her children, the professional would be rightly concerned if she unexpectedly decided that she no longer wanted custody. Such an abrupt change of heart should lead to an investigation of the client's decision.

2. Can the client explain the rationale for her decision or preference?

One typical characteristic of a self-determined decision or preference is that the individual can explain the rationale. If a client is unable to justify her decision, it may be that she has not carefully thought through the options or she is following the wishes of another individual.

Asking the client to explain her reasoning process also assists in determining whether she is making a decision based upon false beliefs. If a client, for example, tells the professional that she wants to surrender custody of her children because she has just discovered that she is HIV-infected, she may be assuming that she will shortly develop AIDS. She may be unaware that although she is HIV-positive, she could live a normal life for many years.

Depending upon the answers to these questions, the professional may need to provide additional information or services to the client. The following case example presents issues related to client self-determination:

Randy has been the caseworker for Darnee and her two children for the last four months. Darnee has adhered to her service plan and has seemed determined to have her children returned to her. In the last month, however, Darnee missed three appointments with her substance abuse counselor and two visits with her children. Darnee did not reply when Randy asked her about the missed appointments. Randy recorded the incidents and began to wonder if an outside factor might be influencing Darnee's behavior because it was inconsistent with her previous work toward the return of her children.

On a home visit, Randy found Darnee arguing with a man. Randy made an appointment with Darnee for the next day. During their conversation, he learned that the man was Darnee's boyfriend, Ray, who had been released from prison two months ago and was living with her. Ray had stolen Darnee's last public aid check and had stolen her bus tokens. As a result, she was not able to keep her appointments with her counselor or with her children. Worse, he had pressured her to use drugs with him, and she now feels ashamed. Randy and Darnee talked about the consequences of the missed appointments and discussed Ray's influence on Darnee. Randy recommended counseling services for domestic violence.

Randy's suspicions that an outside factor was affecting Darnee's self-determination (because missing appointments was inconsistent with her previously expressed values and behavior) were correct. Once Randy uncovered the influence that Ray was having on Darnee, he was able to take steps to enhance Darnee's ability to be self-determining. He discussed with Darnee the consequences of her actions, and he offered her appropriate services.

When working with clients, the child welfare professional must maximize opportunities for self-determination. After providing information and eliminating factors that limit self-determination to the extent it is possible to do so, the professional likely will have his or her own opinion about the choices the client should make. Nevertheless, the choice is the client's to make, and, inevitably, clients will make choices that the professional judges to be poor or wrong. Professionals must accept the client's choice, and, if necessary, proceed accordingly, such as by recording nonattendance at mandated programs and reporting noncooperation to the court. Using the previous example, if Darnee decides that she cannot live without Ray and continues to be influenced by him, she may lose custody of her children on a permanent basis. Randy's role can extend only to advising her of the consequences if she makes such choices and offering her services to help her avoid those consequences.

CHILDREN AND SELF-DETERMINATION

Special issues regarding client self-determination are presented when the client is a minor. To what degree should children be allowed to make their own decisions? The issue of children and self-determination is complicated. It should not be assumed that children cannot make any self-determined choices, but there obviously are significant limits to a child's capacity to make certain decisions. The guiding principle that child welfare professionals should follow is that all clients, whatever their age, should have the opportunity to make self-determined choices according to their level of understanding and decisionmaking capacity.

Whenever possible, the wishes of children should be determined and taken into consideration. Although their choices or preferences may not be in their best interest, it is nonetheless important to give weight to what the child wishes. The child's desires are particularly important as the age (or maturity) of the child increases; when there is significant disagreement among the professionals involved about the child's best interest; or when the choice to be made will have a significant long-term impact on the child's life. The following case illustrates these considerations:

> Thomas is 8 years old. He is currently placed with his maternal aunt who also has custody of four of his siblings. Thomas's aunt, age 57, has said that she does not want to adopt Thomas because she is already overwhelmed with the responsibility for so many children. Another family has seen Thomas's photo in the state's adoption photo listing

book, and they have asked that he be placed with them on a preadoptive basis. Thomas's caseworker feels that the placement would give Thomas opportunities that are not available at his aunt's home. Thomas, however, feels strongly that he does not want to leave his aunt and his siblings.

Because of Thomas's age and the impact that this decision would have on his life, his caseworker must take Thomas's opinion into consideration. The impact on Thomas could be negative if the agency grants his wish to stay with his aunt and siblings and his aunt finds herself unable to manage the five children. The caseworker might consider other options that would honor Thomas' desire to remain close to his siblings and aunt. In formulating these options, the caseworker should consider the following:

- Would Thomas feel better about living with another family if he knew he would visit his aunt regularly?

- Where does the prospective adoptive family live? Do they live near Thomas' aunt?

- Would the family also consider adopting one or more of Thomas's siblings so that he would not be alone?

- Are there other families in the aunt's neighborhood or church who would be interested in caring for Thomas or one or more of his siblings so that the burden on the aunt would be lessened?

- What should the response be if Thomas will not accept any of the alternative options to remaining with his aunt?

To the extent that a child has the capacity to be self-determining, every effort should be made to respect the child's self-determination. It may not always be possible to allow children to be self-determining. There are situations in which youth are allowed to make too many of their own decisions when they need authoritative oversight and direction. The following example illustrates this issue:

> Kristen is 16 and has one child who is 2 years old. Kristen was placed in foster care at age 15, and at her own insistence, was placed in an independent living arrangement. Kristen's caseworker, Marge, visits her once a month and reminds her to keep her apartment clean. Kristen has not been going to school and, unbeknownst to Marge, has been engaging in prostitution to earn money to support her boyfriend's drug habit. The boyfriend has moved into her apartment.

Given Kristen's apparent inability to make decisions in her own best interest, allowing her to do as she pleases in an independent living situation does not respect her self-determination. Deferring to Kristen's desires, in fact, creates a harmful situation for Kristen and her child. Her very lack of judgment inhibits her self-determination.

OVERRIDING CLIENTS' CHOICES

There are situations when a child welfare professional must intercede and override a client's decision. These situations may involve a risk of harm to a child, the client, or others.

Protecting a Child

Because the primary purpose of the child welfare system is to protect children, the self-determination of an adult client can always be overridden to protect the child client. Indeed, it is because of this very principle that children enter the child welfare system. Similarly, a child's choices or preferences can be overridden when she poses a threat to herself. For example, a child's wish to return home to an abusive parent should not be honored. In such cases, deferring to the child's wish does not reflect respect for client self-determination but instead allows the child to be harmed by her lack of decision-making capacity.

Protecting an Adult Client

Interference in a client's decision also may be required when an adult client poses a serious threat to himself. Just as a child's decision may be overridden if the decision would result in harm to that child, the same line of reasoning can, with some caution, be used with regard to adult clients. Respect for self-determination usually overrides a threat of harm when the client himself is the only person who stands to be harmed. It is generally agreed, however, that a professional should intervene if the client self-mutilates or is suicidal. Part of the rationale for intervention in such situations is that the client is not truly self-determining at the time that he engages in such behavior. If, for example, it appears that a client is suicidal as a result of depression, the depression may be directing his action and he may not be self-determining.

Protecting a Nonclient

Because clients do not have the right to harm others, a professional may be permitted to override the decisions, preferences, or actions of a client when it appears that the client poses a threat to an outside party. This decision is not easily made and will be discussed later in Chapter 4.

WHAT IS INFORMED CONSENT?

Informed consent requires professionals to inform clients of probable outcomes of the available alternatives before they consent to a treatment or a program. Informed consent emanates from the principle of client self-determination. It is based on the provision of complete and accurate information regarding the nature of the intervention and a discussion between the professional and the client about the possible consequences of that intervention. In voluntary circumstances, clients seek out the services of the professional, and through informed consent, make choices about participation in services. Child welfare professionals have the responsibility to engage in the process of information sharing and discussion of consequences with mandated clients. Although these clients have not chosen to become clients, they have options to consider and decisions to make within the framework of mandated intervention.

Informed consent can be understood in the context of medical care. When an individual sees a doctor, he wants to know about the medications and treatments the doctor recommends: What will the treatment be like? How much time will it take? What side effects can be expected? What is the likelihood that the treatment will help and to what degree? Patients also want to know the options and their consequences so that they can choose the treatment that best suits their needs, or, alternatively, decide to forego treatment altogether. Mandated clients in the child welfare system deserve to be similarly informed.

In child welfare, clients typically are forced into contact with the agency and are subject to the agency's decisions and actions. Child welfare clients do not have the freedom to withdraw from services without negative consequences, such as removal of children from their custody or the termination of their parental rights. The Illinois *Code of Ethics for Child Welfare Professionals* defines informed consent in the context of child welfare as follows:

> Child welfare professionals should inform clients as soon as feasible and in language that is understandable about the nature of the professional relationship, the nature of the professional intervention, the professional's delegated authority and the limits of that authority, which decisions the client can make, and which decisions the child welfare professionals will make.

> Child welfare professionals should inform clients of the role of the court, if any, and of their legal and procedural rights.

> Child welfare professionals should keep clients informed about the case plan throughout the entire intervention.

Child welfare professionals should obtain permission for intervention from a legally authorized person when a client is legally incapable of giving informed consent.

Child welfare professionals should seek assent for intervention from clients who are not capable of giving an informed consent, giving due consideration to the clients' preferences in pursuing their best interests.

The key elements of informed consent are the following:

- An absence of coercion and undue influence.

- A description of anticipated costs to the client and significant others.

- The capability of the client to provide consent.

- A clear and complete explanation (in the client's native language and at his or her level of comprehension) of suggested aims and methods, including the purposes of the methods.

- A description of possible discomforts and risks (including effects on the client's job, family, and independence).

- A description of hoped-for benefits.

- A description of alternative service methods and their potential goals, benefits, and risks.

- An offer to answer any questions.

- A statement that the client is free to withdraw consent and discontinue participation at any time (although it is important to communicate in the child welfare setting that a withdrawal could result in the loss of custody of the client's children).

FOUR IMPORTANT THEMES OF INFORMED CONSENT

Client consent is authentic when the client is fully informed about service options, the client is competent to give consent, consent is voluntary, and consent is based on a clear understanding of options.

Full Information About Options

Consent is truly informed only when clients have been given information about their options and the consequences of each option. Research shows that even in voluntary settings, informed consent requirements are often not followed (Lidz, et al. 1984). In a study of 540 psychiatrists from 94 state and country mental hospitals in 35 states, only 54% of psychiatrists told their patients about the irreversible risks of a certain medication although statutes required psychiatrists to disclose them (Kennedy & Sanborn, 1992). In mandated settings such as child welfare, it is even easier to avoid providing informed consent.

As a starting point, child welfare professionals should accurately represent their personal qualifications, including competence, to their clients, agencies, and the public. The professional should be thoroughly knowledgeable about the field as such professional knowledge is a requisite to providing clients with the opportunity for informed consent. If a professional does not know about various alternatives ("what's out there"), she cannot inform her clients about the available options. All child welfare professionals, especially supervisors and administrators, should remain current on the research on service options.

Informed consent requires a clear description of alternatives in relation to the desired outcome and the potential effectiveness of each alternative. If, for example, a child welfare professional is working with a parent whom she believes lacks parenting skills, she will want to refer her client to a parent training program that has been evaluated and shown to be effective. Some parent training programs have been found to be helpful (Macdonald, 2000); others have been found to be quite ineffective (that is, participants' parenting skills decline); and many programs have not been evaluated at all. In thinking critically about available parenting training programs, the child welfare professional should ask:

- Has this program been critically evaluated, and if so, what are the results?

- Was it found to be effective or ineffective?

- Have other types of parent training programs been evaluated and found to be helpful? If so, why are these programs not being used for the agency's clients?

- Should clients be informed about the other types of programs that are available?

Clients want this type of information. In one study, clients were asked which criteria they would like professionals to use in selecting methods to help them. Clients identified as important both the professional's track record in using a method successfully and the research evidence about the methods (O'Donohue, Fisher, & Plaud, 1989).

Although information on program effectiveness is important, child welfare professionals may question if it is really necessary and may raise issues about exactly how much information should be provided. There are three common justifications for failing to provide such information. The first two justifications are related.

First, child welfare professionals may believe that they should have full discretion with regard to the type of information that is communicated to clients. Second, child welfare professionals may believe that fully informing clients will create positive expectations or a placebo effect that has no relationship to actual improvement. Staff, for example, may know that the assessment methods they or referral agencies use are not likely to produce accurate information. Caseworkers, as a result, may base referrals of clients to parent training programs solely on parents' self-reports regarding how they interact with their children rather than on any assessment information that they receive. The parenting program may not provide the services that the client really needs, but the child welfare professional may hope that despite the likely mismatch, the client will improve her parenting skills because she expects to do so.

These two objections conflict with the principle that providing full information is an ethical obligation in obtaining informed consent. In some situations, professional discretion and commitment to the client's best interest may justify a child welfare professional's decision to limit the type or amount of information that she provides to a client. The professional, however, would be on ethically tenuous ground if she withholds information from a competent client for the client's "own good." The presumption must be that the client should receive as much information as possible unless there is a strong justification to the contrary.

The third justification for failing to provide information is that caseworkers often have little time to obtain the information and disclose all of the facts and potential consequences of possible treatments and service plan options. A child welfare professional must identify what information needs to be disclosed and what information does not need to be disclosed. One standard for making such decisions is the "reasonable person standard" which requires a professional to provide the amount and type of information a reasonable person would want to know before consenting (or withholding consent) to participate in a particular program. Although this criterion provides a helpful benchmark for child welfare professionals, it is only a starting point. Professionals should add to the basic information what a reasonable person would require based on the client's own particular characteristics or history or based on other factors. A reasonable person, for example, may not need to know whether a particular program offers parenting classes in Spanish, but such information would be very important to a Spanish-speaking client.

Competence to Give Informed Consent

Consent is informed only when a client is competent to give consent. The standard for determining competence is not clear. One simple standard is the capacity to express a preference. This minimal standard requires very little as an individual who is not capable of understanding the basic facts about her circumstances and the consequences of her decision nonetheless can express a preference. A higher standard requires the capacity to offer some justification for one's preference. An even more stringent standard requires the capacity to offer a reasoned preference on the basis of an understanding of the risks and benefits of alternatives (Beauchamp & Childress, 1989) and to compare alternatives on the basis of risks and benefits (Ozar and Sokol, 1984).

The capacity to make decisions is task-specific. As a result, a determination of competence requires the use of criteria that are flexible enough to take the type of decision into consideration. Simply because someone has difficulty maintaining a job, for example, it should not be assumed that she is incapable of choosing among drug rehabilitation programs. Conversely, simply because someone is highly competent in certain aspects of her life, it should not be assumed that she is competent to make all types of decisions. As a general rule, however, the greater the consequence of a decision, the greater the competence or decisionmaking capability that is required. Because there is very little at stake, inconsequential decisions do not require much in the way of decisionmaking capacity. Decisions of great consequence, however, must be addressed more carefully, and the professional should ensure that the client has the ability to understand the likely consequences of his decision. A decision that may prevent a parent from being reunited with his children, for example, requires great care. Decisionmaking deficiencies that may be tolerated when less important decisions are required should not be allowed to affect important decisions. When a client is not capable of making decisions or participating in the decisionmaking process (as is the case with infants and young children), others must make decisions based upon what they believe is in that person's best interest.

Voluntariness of the Decision

The third element of informed consent is that the decision is voluntary. Voluntariness refers to a client's freedom from coercion or manipulation in making decisions, such as, for child welfare clients, choices about the case plan. Coercion limits a client's choices by forcing them into situations that the caseworker chooses. A caseworker, for example, may refuse to take children to visit at the location chosen by the parent, forcing the parent to accept the location that the caseworker has chosen. Like coercion, manipulation inhibits the voluntariness of clients' decisions. Manipulation differs from coercion in that it does not involve an explicit act of limiting choices but rather relies upon forms of control which allow the client to feel as if she has made a voluntary choice. Manipulation involves offering of choices in such a way that the client is led to choose a particular option. Manipulation may be informational, as when a caseworker deliberately does not mention a certain treatment program because he does not want the client to choose it. Most often, however, manipulation is less obvious. A caseworker may deliberately describe some programs in a positive way and some in a negative way so that the client will be more likely to choose certain programs (Beauchamp & Childress, 1989). Similarly, a caseworker may become irritated if a client asks for information about a program that the caseworker does not wish to offer, and the client may not pursue the issue for fear of alienating the caseworker.

Understanding

Disclosure of information will not result in informed consent unless the client understands the information that has been disclosed. It is important to view the disclosure of information not simply as a procedure to be followed but as a way to enhance the client's understanding of his situation. The child welfare professional must present information in a way that is understandable to the client. Needless technical jargon should be avoided; the client's questions should be answered; and the client should be given adequate time to process information. Clients often have difficulty comprehending and appreciating large or complicated pieces of information. As a result, the professional should be available by telephone or other means to answer client's questions as they arise.

WAYS OF PROVIDING INFORMATION

Clients can be informed in a number of ways. The most common approach is simply to talk to the client about the available options. A client, for example, may be court-ordered to participate in counseling. The child welfare professional might discuss with the client the type of counselor with whom the client would like to work and the benefits and disadvantages of working with different types of counselors. The professional might advise a young mother that she may be more comfortable talking with a female counselor and, as a result, may derive greater benefit from her sessions; or alternatively, the professional might point out that the male counselor who is available has more experience with the types of issues that are causing the client the greatest distress. If the professional has difficulty talking with the client, it may helpful to ask her supervisor to join the discussion.

There are several other alternatives that professionals can utilize to provide clients with full information about service alternatives. One approach is to have the client meet with service providers and ask the providers to explain the benefits of their services. Another alternative is to develop brochures that provide full information (such as hours of operation, extent of service flexibility, success rates, and related research findings) about each of the programs that provide services. Third, it may be helpful to arrange for a client to talk to peers who have participated in various programs. If professionals have difficulty obtaining an adequate level of information about the various programs that provide services to agency clients, it may be useful to form an advocacy group or monitoring panel that could obtain information for clients who need to make decisions about services in an informed manner.

SUMMARY

A child welfare client has the right of self-determination within the limits of the involuntary setting. The professional can assist the client in making appropriate decisions and enhance client self-determination by providing sufficient information about options and addressing any factors that could inhibit self-determination. Table 3-1 summarizes the factors that may affect client self-determination and effective ways to address those factors. When clients make self-determined decisions, those decisions should be respected. There may be justification for overriding the client's decision only when there is a threat of harm to the child, an adult client, or to others.

An important application of respect for client self-determination is that of informed consent. The four elements of informed consent are: disclosure of information (which includes the available alternatives, the consequences of each alternative, the track record of each program alternative, and the results of evaluations of the effectiveness of program); client competence (which is task-specific and must be determined based on the importance of the decision); voluntariness (that is, decisions free from coercion and/or manipulation); and the client's understanding of the information.

Table 3-1. Factors that Limit Self-Determination and Techniques for Addressing Those Factors

Factors that Limit Self-Determination

- Lack of information, false information, or false beliefs
- Diminished cognitive capacity
- The complexity of the child welfare system
- Language difficulty
- Mental illness
- Reaction to the mandated situation
- Psychosocial factors

Techniques for Addressing Factors that Limit Self-Determination

- Encourage the client to explain the rationale behind her decision.
- Encourage the client to explain the options in his own words.
- When a decision is of great consequence, allow sufficient time for the client to consider the issue and change his or her mind. Periodically ask the client if she continues to feel the same way about the issue
- Be alert for decisions or preferences that are out of character (that is, inconsistent with what appear to be the client's usual values).
- Avoid holding important conversations in anxiety-producing environments; after the client has received upsetting news; or in the presence of others who might unduly influence the client's decisions.
- Manage time carefully and in an organized manner so that sufficient time may be spent with clients and there are opportunities to adequately inform clients about their options.
- Maintain a demeanor that encourages communication so that clients are not fearful of asking questions.
- Take steps to reduce unreasonable caseloads so that an appropriate amount of time may be spent with each client.
- Avoid needless flowery vocabulary and technical jargon. Do not put clients in the embarrassing position of having to ask for explanations of the words being used.

CASE STUDIES FOR CHAPTER 3

Case Study 3-1. Belin is 11 years old and does not want to visit with her mother. Belin is stubborn and simply refuses to go to the visits. When the last visit was scheduled, she ran away for the afternoon. What should Belin's caseworker do?

Case Study 3-2. Josh is the caseworker for Cathy. Cathy's 5-year-old son was severely burned after hot water was spilled on him in the family kitchen. Cathy's children were removed from her custody after a series of similar incidents. When Josh talked with Cathy, he noticed that she was slow to answer and that she asked him to repeat information several times. She had great difficulty understanding what he said. Should Josh be concerned about Cathy's self-determination? What questions should Josh ask?

Case Study 3-3. Charmane is a child protective services investigator. She visits the Perez household on an allegation of neglect after the school social worker made a report that the two Perez children seemed to be malnourished. Charmane explains to Mrs. Perez that she could apply for public benefits and food stamps and avoid the possibility that her children would be placed in foster care. Mrs. Perez is a U.S. citizen, but she appears afraid and refuses to go to the public benefits office. Could there be other factors affecting Mrs. Perez's decision? If so, what might they be? What should Charmane do?

Case Study 3-4. Jordan is a new case manager for the Theta Agency. He has assumed responsibility for a number of cases, one of which involves Terry, a mildly retarded 17-year-old ward. Because Terry has a history of being easily coerced into inappropriate behavior, Jordan's supervisor believes that Terry should be withdrawn from school and enrolled in a GED program. What questions should Jordan ask about Terry's situation?

Case Study 3-5. Tami is a new caseworker. One of her first clients is Liz. Liz has been ordered by the court to participate in a drug treatment program. Tami locates such a program near Liz's house, gives Liz the address, and tells her that she must attend that program. Has Tami obtained informed consent from Liz? What else could she have done?

Case Study 3-6. The caseworkers at XYZ Agency routinely refer clients to a parent training program that does not conduct individual assessments of clients enrolled in the program. Instead, the program offers one training package for all parents. What are the ethical issues that this situation raises? What should the staff at the agency do?

Case Study 3-7. Henry is Beth's caseworker. He refers Beth to a substance abuse treatment program, but he does not tell her that the program is known to keep very poor records about clients' progress. He is concerned that if Beth knows about the problems with the program, she will lose hope that she can change her drug behavior. He believes that the information would interfere with her expectations of success. What issues does Henry's decision raise?

Case Study 3-8. Alana is a very busy caseworker and is running late for her next appointment. Her client, Lisa, needs to begin parenting classes. Alana knows that there are three programs in Lisa's neighborhood. She quickly mentions them and asks Lisa to choose one. Alana does not say whether there are any differences among the three programs. Can Lisa give informed consent?

Case Study 3-9. Patty, a child welfare caseworker, had a romantic relationship with Mike, a substance abuse counselor at the Ita Agency. Since Mike ended the relationship, Patti has been trying to devise ways to contact him. Patty's newest client, Regi, must enroll in a substance abuse program. Patty tells Regi about different program alternatives, but she emphasizes that the Ita Agency has, by far, the best services. Can Regi make a voluntary choice in this situation?

Case Study 3-10. Olsen referred his client to a parent-training program that research suggests will be effective if implemented as designed. Olsen does not know how well the staff implements the program nor does he have any idea about the agency's record of success in helping individuals similar to his client. Is Olsen's client able to give informed consent under these circumstances?

Case Study 3-11. Melody, a unit supervisor, has met with her staff twice to discuss their obligations to fully inform clients about how they choose assessment, intervention, and evaluation methods for their clients. The staff realize that they often make decisions based on what resources are available, intuition, and what they hear from colleagues rather than on what research suggests is best. The caseworkers disagree about the appropriate criteria that should be used to select service methods. In the meantime, clients remain uninformed. What should Melody do?

Chapter 4

Confidentiality

Confidentiality is the ethical value that requires the protection of information that is shared within the professional-client relationship. Child welfare professionals have access to sensitive information that must be kept confidential to protect and respect the clients with whom they work or consult. Not only does the law often require that confidentiality be maintained in child welfare, but confidentiality allows trust to develop in the worker-client relationship and, in turn, makes professional practice possible. Establishing this trust, however, may be complicated because child welfare professionals must report clients' actions to the court as a means of protecting children and complying with state law.

Child welfare professionals must carry out varying and often conflicting responsibilities to their clients, the courts, and in some cases, other parties. As a result, they should have a clear understanding of confidentiality laws, including the type of information that they may justifiably share and with whom they may share such information. This chapter discusses the importance of maintaining confidentiality, the limits of confidentiality, and the circumstances under which a breach of confidentiality may be justified.

CONFIDENTIALITY LAW

A child welfare professional's responsibility to maintain confidentiality requires that she not divulge to an outside party any information received from a client unless the client consents. In general, client information is confidential as to outside inquiries and may be justifiably shared with others only when the information is necessary to fulfill the professional's responsibility to the client. In each state, there are laws that prescribe specific limits regarding confidentiality. These laws may address confidentiality requirements in such areas as child abuse and neglect reporting, the provision of child welfare services, mental health and developmental disabilities services, and HIV/AIDS. Child welfare professionals should be familiar with these requirements and should seek the guidance of their supervisors if they have questions about the legal requirements related to confidentiality.

JUSTIFYING CONFIDENTIALITY

Confidentiality is a value that lies at the core of the child welfare profession. Child welfare professionals should respect the confidentiality rights of clients and those with whom they work or consult. The approaches to ethical decisionmaking discussed in Chapter One—the ethical standards approach and the outcomes approach—provide a basis for justifying confidentiality as a core child welfare value.

When the ethical standards approach is utilized, confidentiality may be seen as an implicit assumption of the professional-client relationship. Without this assumption, clients would not trust professionals and would not speak openly. From this perspective, breaching confidentiality violates ethical standards but is ultimately unethical because it betrays the client's trust and violates the responsibilities of the fiduciary relationship. Maintaining confidentiality also demonstrates respect for the client's inherent dignity because it allows the client to control the information that is made available about herself.

Finally, the ethical standards approach suggests that the justification for confidentiality may be framed in terms of rights. Viewed in this way, a person has a right to confidentiality based on a right to privacy which, in turn, is justified by a more general right to self-determination. A right to self-determination entails, among other things, the right to control the nature and amount of information made available about oneself.

When the outcomes approach is utilized, confidentiality may be justified on the basis of the therapeutic importance of a client's ability to speak openly within the professional-client relationship. If clients fear that a professional will disclose sensitive information to outside parties, they will be reluctant to speak freely. The negative outcome will be the weakening of the client's trust and the weakening of the professional-client relationship. In turn, the professional's effectiveness will be hampered.

This discussion should not be taken to suggest that client information should never be shared. Maintaining absolute confidentiality would debilitate the child welfare system and could cause harm to both clients and nonclients. In many cases, sensitive information about a client must be shared.

THE LIMITS OF CONFIDENTIALITY IN CHILD WELFARE

Within the child welfare system, sharing information obtained from clients is regularly required. It is important that professionals understand the reasons behind the justifiable sharing of information as these reasons clarify the limits of confidentiality. When the professional clearly understands the limits of confidentiality, she will be better able to communicate those limits to her clients. It is extremely important that child welfare professionals discuss the limits of confidentiality with clients at the outset of the relationship.

There are six common reasons that child welfare professionals share client information with others:

1. *To effectively provide services to the client.* It often is necessary for a caseworker to share certain information about a client with others, including supervisors, other agencies and individuals providing services, foster parents, and the courts. Information is shared to ensure that comprehensive services are provided to the client. Information also may be shared in order to protect the child. Because the best interest of the child is the priority, there will be times when the caseworker must recommend that a child not be returned home. The caseworker often must use client-provided information in her court testimony to justify her recommendation.

2. *To enable the foster parent to parent effectively.* Foster parents must know the social history and the medical and psychological needs of the children for whom they are caring. Such information as the child's prenatal drug exposure or the child's history of sex abuse should be provided. This information may unavoidably reveal information about a birthparent as well. Only information about the parent that is relevant to the foster parent's role in caring for the child, however, should be revealed.

3. *To protect other children in the foster home.* Another reason to share confidential information with foster parents (or with the staff of residential facilities) is to protect other children in the home or facility. If, for example, a child tends to behave in ways that may pose a threat to other children, this information must be shared. Only relevant information should be shared and only with those individuals who have direct "need to know."

4. *To protect the child welfare professional.* There are situations that require that information be shared to protect the child welfare professional. A client, for example, may file a lawsuit against the professional or against the agency. The professional may need to disclose information about the client in order to legally protect herself or the agency.

5. *To protect outside parties (nonclients).* It may become necessary to share information about a client to protect innocent third parties. If a client poses a threat to an outside party, the professional may have a duty to warn that individual. This issue will be discussed more fully later in this chapter.

6. *To comply with the law or agency policy.* In certain situations, child welfare professionals are required by law or by agency policy to disclose information about their clients. In most states, for example, child welfare professionals are required to report suspected child abuse.

The following case raises issues about sharing client information:

> Kelly is the substance abuse counselor for Leyla. Leyla had been in recovery for five months when she has a relapse. Kelly discovers the situation on a home visit. Leyla begs Kelly not to tell her caseworker because she is afraid the relapse would further delay the return of her children to her custody. Kelly is uncertain how she should handle the situation and wonders whether, if she informs Leyla's caseworker about the incident, she would breach confidentiality.

In this situation, Kelly should talk to Leyla's caseworker about the incident because the caseworker needs such information in order to make the best possible decisions about Leyla and her children. The consequences of the relapse may not be as serious as Leyla believes. The caseworker, in fact, may understand that relapse is quite common during recovery. Simply because Leyla has asked Kelly to keep a secret does not mean that Kelly should keep that information in confidence, nor does it mean that she is breaching confidentiality if she shares it with Leyla's caseworker. The situation could have been avoided if Kelly had explained the limits of confidentiality at the outset of their relationship.

INFORMING THE CLIENT OF THE LIMITS OF CONFIDENTIALITY

Limits of confidentiality refer to the points at which a professional can no longer maintain confidentiality. One area in which there are limits of confidentiality for child welfare professionals involves the professional's responsibility to advise the court about the client's progress. The child welfare professional should discuss this responsibility with the client at the outset of the relationship and ensure that the client understands that information will be shared with the court. This discussion is based on the professional's respect for the right of clients to be informed about their situation. It also acknowledges that even when a client may not want information shared, she should, at the very least, be made aware of what information will be shared with whom.

There may be other instances when client information may need to be shared with others. It is important that the professionals clarify their relationship with the client and clearly communicate that certain information will not be kept in confidence. In such situations, the professional may share certain information outside the relationship without violating confidentiality. The client will be less likely to feel betrayed and the child welfare professional will be better able to retain client trust. Ideally, clients should sign a release, authorizing the professional to share information about themselves with others. In cases in which the client refuses to sign an authorization to release information, the client should be informed that his refusal may appear noncompliant and may further delay the return of his children to him or make their return home less likely.

A child welfare professional may encounter obstacles to her efforts to effectively inform a client about the limits of confidentiality. The client may have diminished cognitive capacities (as may be the case when a client has engaged in long-term substance abuse) and may not understand or appreciate the limits of confidentiality. In such cases, the worker should take steps to protect the client and himself by making repeated attempts to clarify the limits in clear simple language that the client can understand; asking the client to bring someone who is willing to be involved in his case and can support him; or contacting the client's lawyer to explain the problem. If the client is a child, there are special issues related to limits of confidentiality. In many states, a child of 12 years of age or older is considered old enough to be legally involved in decision-making concerning his future. In these cases, the child's confidentiality rights and the limits of confidentiality should be discussed with him.

When it is necessary to disclose information about a client, the child welfare professional should disclose the least amount of identifying information that is necessary, based on the purpose of the disclosure.

PROTECTING WHAT IS CONFIDENTIAL

A breach of confidentiality means that a professional has shared information the client had good reason to believe would be kept in confidence. When the limits of confidentiality are not discussed with a client, an appropriate sharing of information becomes a breach of confidentiality because the client justifiably feels betrayed. In child welfare, most breaches of confidentiality occur because child welfare professionals do not have a clear understanding of when they may justifiably share information. When sharing information is neither necessary to provide effective services nor to protect individuals from harm, the information must be kept confidential and should not be shared.

Common ways that confidentiality is breached are through faxing confidential files; leaving files in common areas; speaking with unauthorized persons (such as family members, neighbors, or reporters) about a client's case; speaking loudly to the client on the phone so that others can overhear; and discussing a case in public places (such as an elevator, hallway, or restaurant). The following guidelines can assist child welfare professionals to avoid inadvertent breaches of confidentiality:

- When talking on the phone, do not discuss the client's case with an unidentified caller. The only callers to whom a professional should speak freely on the tele-

phone are social service providers with whom the professional is working directly in the service of the client and representatives of the child welfare agency. If a
caller claims to have a right to information, the professional should consult with
her supervisor and/or agency policy to verify the caller's authorization. If uncertainty remains, the caller should be asked to provide a release signed by the client,
the child's guardian, or another designee.

- When leaving a message for a client at the client's home, do not leave confidential information on an answering machine or as a message with another person.

- When talking with a client, ensure that the office door is closed so that others
  cannot overhear the conversation.

- When in public places (such as elevators, hallways, and restaurants), never discuss
  cases.

- When in the office, do not talk to individuals who present themselves asking for
  information, such as reporters, employers, family, or neighbors of the client
  unless they are cleared by a supervisor.

- When using fax machines, do not fax confidential information unless it is
  absolutely necessary because of time constraints. If documents must be faxed
  immediately, use a "CONFIDENTIAL" cover sheet. Always double-check fax
  numbers to minimize the chance that confidential information could be faxed to
  the wrong location. When faxing confidential material, always call first so that the
  receiving party can wait for its arrival.

- When using cell phones, avoid discussing client information because of the possibility that cell phone communications can be intercepted.

- When using e-mail, avoid sending confidential information. E-mails may be
  intercepted, sent to the wrong location, or opened by unauthorized persons.

- When handling mental health, HIV, or substance abuse information, consult the
  American Medical Association for proper protocol in keeping records and disclosing information.

- Do not leave documents containing confidential information open on computer
  screens.

- Never leave confidential material lying open on a desk.

- Whenever possible, get signed consent forms and keep them on file.

If these guidelines designed to protect client information are not followed, a professional may breach confidentiality unintentionally. The following example illustrates such a situation:

> Dawn is a caseworker. One day, a man calls her office. He does not identify himself and begins asking questions about one of Dawn's clients, Jeannie. Dawn often speaks by telephone to Jeannie's drug counselor, parent-training professional, and parole officer about Jeannie's case. Caught off guard, Dawn acknowledges to the caller that Jeannie is in drug treatment. The man is a prospective employer who is considering Jeannie for a position. He had heard a rumor that Jeannie has been a drug addict and has lost custody of her child. He called the agency to confirm this information before hiring her.

In this case, Dawn has breached confidentiality. She should have asked the man to identify himself before acknowledging that Jeannie was a client. If any uncertainty remained, Dawn should have asked the caller to provide a release signed by Jeannie that would authorize her to discuss any matters concerning Jeannie. Dawn also may have opted to first contact Jeannie to obtain her consent to speak with the caller.

Although child welfare professionals should respect confidentiality, keeping confidentiality cannot be an ethical absolute. Maintaining confidentiality, for example, may cause serious harm to others. In such instances, the child welfare professional (along with her supervisor) may struggle with the ethical dilemma of whether to share confidential information in order to avoid possible harm to others.

DELIBERATELY BREACHING CONFIDENTIALITY

Most deliberate breaches of confidentiality are highly unethical. Sometimes, however, child welfare and professionals and their agencies may have an ethical reason to consider a deliberate breach of confidentiality. A client or a third party may be at risk of harm that could be prevented if the professional were to breach confidentiality. These situations may give rise to the "duty to warn," that is, the obligation to warn an individual whom the professional knows to be in danger.

In 1976, the famous *Tarasoff* case was decided in California. In this case, the court found that the therapist of the boyfriend of a murder victim had a duty to warn the victim or her family that she was in danger. The court found that the therapist was legally liable for failing to do so. Subsequently, legislation was enacted in many states regarding professionals' duty to warn. In some states, the law mandates that social workers and therapists report to a third party when that party is in danger, and in other states, the law simply offers protection from liability to social workers and therapists if they choose to do so.

Any decision to breach confidentiality will have legal implications. Some breaches of confidentiality are legally permitted if not required, and other breaches of confidentiality are specifically prohibited by law. Because the law varies from one state to another, a professional who is considering breaching confidentiality should discuss the situation with her supervisor, legal counsel, the agency board, and/or ethics committee. The following example illustrates some of the issues that a professional may face when he considers whether to deliberately breach confidentiality:

> Emma's three children were taken into protective custody after it was determined that the children had been seriously neglected. The children are now living with Emma's mother-in-law, but the goal is return home to Emma. Through the help of Brad, her caseworker, Emma has completed a substance abuse rehabilitation program, and through counseling, she has been addressing her depression and her anger at her estranged husband. Emma has passed each drug test over the past seven months. She also has received a promotion at work. Brad feels that Emma is basically a very loving mother but that the pressure and circumstances surrounding her separation from her husband have overwhelmed her and led to substance abuse. Brad is proud of Emma's progress, and Emma recognizes that she owes a great deal to Brad's professional commitment. Brad feels confident that Emma's children will be returned to her. He has reassured her on several occasions that she will succeed in this regard.
>
> Emma was recently informed that her estranged husband is filing for divorce and is seeking custody of their children. On his last visit, Brad found her extremely angry and depressed. Emma stated several times that she fantasized about killing her husband. Brad was able to calm her, but he left her home feeling uneasy. The next day, Brad had a message on his voice mail from Emma in which she tearfully and angrily repeated her desire to kill her husband.

In determining whether Brad would be justified in sharing the information that Emma revealed to him, it is helpful to consider five factors:

1. **The degree of potential harm that could result from keeping the information secret.**

The child welfare professional should share client information when significant harm would result if the information were not divulged. The greater the degree of harm that could result from maintaining confidentiality, the greater the justification for breaching it. Because of the fundamental importance of confidentiality to the professional-client relationship, the types of harm that could lead to a justifiable breach in confidentiality tend to be such basic harms as the threat of serious physical injury or death. A potential harm must be significant enough to outweigh the overall importance of confidentiality. The degree of potential harm in this case, a threat to kill to Emma's husband, is a basic harm.

2. **The probability that harm will occur.**

Another important variable is the probability that the harm will occur. Although Emma's threat obviously poses a high degree of potential harm, the probability that Emma will follow through on her remarks is not clear. Brad may need additional information to determine how serious she is. When the degree of potential harm is high, however, the probability needed to justify breaching confidentiality decreases. As a result, when there is a threat to kill a third party, a breach in confidentiality may be justified even when there is a relatively low probability that the harm will occur. By contrast, when the harm is relatively minor (for example, if Emma threatened to break her husband's car window), it becomes more difficult to justify breaching confidentiality even if there is a certainty that the individual will follow through on her threat. Unless the harm itself is significant enough to outweigh the overall importance of confidentiality, the probability that the harm will occur will be of consequence.

The two factors of degree of potential harm and probability that the harm will occur should be considered together when a decision must be made whether to disclose client information. If the potential harm is great and the probability of its occurrence is likewise great, there is a strong justification for breaching confidentiality. Conversely, if the potential harm and probability of its occurrence are both minimal, the justification for breaching confidentiality is weak. The difficult cases occur when there is a high degree of potential harm but a low probability of potential harm, or there is a low degree of potential harm but a high probability of occurrence. When the probability of harm is intermediate, decisions are even less clear cut. Nonetheless, the strength of the justification to breach confidentiality might be charted as follows:

Strong Justification	High Probability of Harm
	High Degree of Harm
	Low Probability of Harm
	High Degree of Harm
Intermediate Situations	
	High Probability of Harm
	Low Degree of Harm
Weak Justification	Low Probability of Harm
	Low Degree of Harm

3. The number of people affected.

A third factor that can be utilized in determining whether to deliberately breach confidentiality is the number of people who could potentially be harmed by maintaining confidentiality. In Emma's case, should she kill her husband, not only would he be harmed, but her children would likely be emotionally harmed.

4. The degree of imminence.

A fourth factor is whether the harm is likely to happen soon. If the potential harm is imminent, the professional will have little time to consider the issue. In Emma's case, there is some reason to believe that she may act on her threats relatively soon given her apparent emotional state.

5. The identifiability of those who could be harmed.

A final factor is the extent to which the persons who stand to be harmed can be specifically identified. In some cases, the threat of harm is vague, that is, not directed at anyone in particular. In the Tarasoff case, the ex-boyfriend specifically told his psychologist that he wanted to kill his girlfriend. In the case example, Emma has specifically threatened to kill her husband. In other cases, the client's threats are not directed at identifiable persons, and consequently, it may be difficult to justify a breach of confidentiality as there is no particular person to warn. In such cases, the degree of potential harm and the likelihood of that harm must be so great that the inability to identify specific people becomes less of an issue. In such cases, the client must pose such a danger to himself or others that he may be involuntarily institutionalized or held by law enforcement authorities.

ALTERNATIVES TO VIOLATING CONFIDENTIALITY

Before concluding that there is justification for revealing client information, a child welfare professional should consider whether there are steps that she could take to avoid having to undermine the trust of a client by sharing information that the client does not want shared. The following steps are sometimes appropriate before intentionally breaching confidentiality:

1. In some situations, it may be possible to persuade the client to disclose information to relevant parties. The professional and the agency must provide the client with support in taking such a step.

2. A professional may offer the client the opportunity to disclose the information with the professional present to provide support.

3. If the professional believes she has reason to disclose information and has been unsuccessful in efforts to support the client to self-disclose, she should inform the client that she is obligated and intends to disclose the information. The professional again should emphasize, as an alternative, that the client can disclose the information himself and confirm with her that the disclosure occurred. This approach can create a somewhat adversarial atmosphere between the professional and the client, and, as a result, the professional should express empathy and support for the client.

Offering these alternatives shows respect for confidentiality and client self-determination because it gives the client options that offer some control over the disclosure of the information. If the client continues to refuse to self-disclose after all options have been offered, the professional should inform the client when she intends to disclose the information, thereby giving the client a final opportunity to self-disclose. With any agreement to self-disclose, the professional should work with the client to confirm that the disclosure has been made.

SUMMARY

Maintaining confidentiality in child welfare is essential. It often is required by law, and, as a result, child welfare professionals should be familiar with confidentiality laws and clearly understand the information that may be justifiably shared and with whom it may be shared. At the same time, maintaining confidentiality allows trust to develop in the professional-client relationship and, in turn, makes professional practice possible. Establishing trust may be complicated in child welfare because of professional responsibilities to report to the court and the need in some cases to share client information with other parties.

There are several possible justifications for sharing client information: to allow service providers to effectively provide services to children and families; to enable foster parents to parent effectively; to protect other children in the foster home, the child welfare professional, or third parties; and to ensure compliance with the law or agency policy. When information is shared among service providers, the professional must inform the client that information will be shared out of necessity but will be kept confidential from persons who do not have a "need to know."

Most breaches of confidentiality result from carelessness and can be prevented by taking precautions. In some cases, there will be a need to consider an intentional breach of confidentiality, such as when the client discloses an intent to harm himself or others. In deciding whether to breach confidentiality, the professional must weigh the degree of potential harm against the likelihood that the harm will occur, as well as consider the number of persons potentially affected, the imminence of the potential harm, and whether there is an identifiable person who could be harmed. In such situations, breaching confidentiality sometimes can be avoided by encouraging the client to disclose the information himself or, if the client refuses to disclose, explaining that the professional will disclose the information at a certain time, thereby providing the client a final opportunity to disclose the information himself.

CASE STUDIES FOR CHAPTER 4

Case Study 4-1. Kiki is in a rush because she is late for an appointment across town. She is en route to a subway stop. Because she needs to talk with her supervisor about a client before her supervisor leaves for vacation that evening, she calls her supervisor on her cell phone. She tells him that she now suspects her client, Sandra, has a mental illness, and she describes Sandra's odd behavior in detail. Has Kiki violated confidentiality?

Case Study 4-2. LeNedra is the caseworker for Cindy. Cindy's neighbor, Mrs. Chin, has heard people fighting in Cindy's apartment and recently heard a rumor that Cindy's children were taken into protective custody. Mrs. Chin telephones LeNedra and asks a number of questions about Cindy and her children. LeNedra tells Mrs. Chin that Cindy's case is confidential and that she cannot discuss any of the details with her. Mrs. Chin tells another neighbor about her conversation with LeNedra, and the neighbor repeats the story to Cindy. Is the way that LeNedra handled Mrs. Chin's call likely to affect Cindy's work with LeNedra? Why or why not?

Case Study 4-3. Lorna is Ellen's case manager. Ellen's children, ages 11 and 4, were removed from her care and placed with their grandmother (Ellen's mother) after it was determined that the children had been neglected. According to the report of the child protective services investigator, Ellen had left the children at home unsupervised for nearly a day and a half. The investigation also revealed evidence of drug use in the home. Lorna has worked hard to gain Ellen's trust and has learned from Ellen that the drug use began as part of her relationship with her previous boyfriend, Tony. When the children entered protective custody, Ellen immediately stopped using drugs and stopped seeing Tony. Tony, however, has begun to call often, asking to see her. Ellen confesses to Lorna that she has met Tony a few times, but she asks Lorna not to mention her meetings with Tony to her mother. Ellen's mother blames Tony for Ellen's current problems, and Ellen has told her mother that she will not see Tony again. Still suspicious, Ellen's mother has asked Lorna if Ellen was seeing Tony, claiming that "as her mother, I have a right to know." What should Lorna do?

Case Study 4-4. Kyle is 11. He has been in a group home since he was 8 years old. Kyle was removed from his parents' custody because of sexual abuse. At the age of 9, he acted out sexually toward another boy in the group home. Since that time, there have been no further incidents, and Kyle has responded very well to therapy. Kyle wants to have a regular foster family and go to a regular school, and Kyle's therapist believes that he is ready for such a placement and that it would be good for him. Who should be informed about Kyle's past? What should they be told?

Case Study 4-5. Janis is an ex-offender with a felony conviction for armed robbery. Her conviction occurred when she was 20, and she is now 32. Are there instances when this information would be relevant to share and other instances when it should be kept confidential?

Case Study 4-6. Kari is the caseworker for Belle. Belle is very isolated and unhappy, and she constantly complains about her sister, Leslie. Belle feels that Leslie has had more advantages than she has had. When anything negative occurs in Belle's life, she blames Leslie and says hateful things about her. Occasionally, Belle has made comments about Leslie that alarm Kari. Kari has sensed from the outset of her relationship with Belle that Belle may have a mental health problem. Belle has refused counseling and repeatedly missed appointments for psychological assessments. Since Belle's parental rights were terminated, she has seemed even more angry and unstable. As she left the courtroom when her parental rights were terminated, Belle flashed Kari a look that Kari considered "scary." Kari is concerned that Belle may do something irrational, and she is very concerned that Belle may attempt to harm Leslie. What should Kari do?

Case Study 4-7. Marvin is in an anger management class. He has become much more aware of how he has used threatening behavior with his family to control them. He has developed a relationship with the instructor, Rachel. One day after class, Marvin approaches Rachel and tells her that he needs to talk. He explains that earlier that week, he lost his job, and when he arrived home, he beat his 13- year-old-son. The son was not severely injured, but he was badly bruised and he ran away from home. Marvin is upset and says he feels out of control and does not know what to do. What should Rachel do?

Case Study 4-8. Jean is a case manager for Sharon and her two children, ages 7 and 5. Sharon has a history of drug abuse, but she successfully completed a rehabilitation program and has regained custody of her children. Sharon recently learned that she is HIV infected. She confides to Jean that she does not want to disclose this information to her current steady boyfriend, Larry, with whom she is sexually active, because she fears he will stop dating her. Sharon hopes that Larry will eventually marry her and help support the family. Larry, who has no children of his own, spends several hours a week in activities with Sharon's children and has a steady job. Jean is proud of Sharon's progress and feels it is her duty to respect Sharon's privacy. Jean considers not telling Larry about Sharon's HIV status, but discusses the issue with her supervisor, Marilyn. Marilyn is extremely busy. She is balancing her school work for her masters degree in social work and her job responsibilities. Marilyn believes that a law prohibits any disclosure of HIV status, and she is aware that no agency policy covers this situation. She does nothing more regarding Jean's question. Soon thereafter, Sharon becomes pregnant with Larry's baby, continues to keep her HIV infection secret, avoids prenatal care, and refuses to attend her Narcotics Anonymous meetings. Sharon is not aware that she should take AZT to lessen the baby's chances being born HIV positive. Jean is aware of AZT therapy and realizes that Sharon does not have this information. She again struggles with whether to disclose Sharon's HIV status. What should Jean do?

Chapter 5

Conflicts of Interest

The media often focuses on conflicts of interest in connection with stories suggesting that government and big business are corrupt. These suspicions may result in public cynicism about the integrity of these organizations and the individuals associated with them. Conflicts of interest also occur in child welfare and, when they do, they can be quite destructive. This chapter defines a conflict of interest, explains why such conflicts present ethical problems, and addresses how conflicts of interest can be prevented. When child welfare professionals have strong skills in analyzing problems that may result in ethical violations, they are better equipped to avoid conflicts of interest that compromise services to their clients and to legally protect their agencies and themselves.

WHAT IS A "CONFLICT OF INTEREST"?

A conflict of interest can be difficult to recognize because the concept often is used to refer to different types of ethical problems. In the context of child welfare, a conflict of interest may be defined as a situation that arises when a professional entrusted to exercise objective judgment in the service of an agency and its clients has an interest that could interfere with the objectivity of that judgment. A conflict of interest has two specific elements, both of which must be present:

1. An individual is entrusted to exercise objective judgment in the service of another party; and

2. The individual has an interest that would lead a reasonable person to believe that the interest would interfere with the objectivity of the professional's judgment, making it less reliable than it would be otherwise.

If one or the other element is not present, an ethical problem may exist, but the problem would not be a conflict of interest and would be addressed differently.

The following vignette raises questions about whether there is a conflict of interest:

Forrest cheats on his timecard because he wants to leave work early to see his son's ball game without losing income.

In this situation, Forrest has a personal interest in seeing his son's game (Element 2), but he is not required to exercise judgment with regard to filling out his time card truthfully (Element 1). This task is simply a policy that he must follow. There is no conflict of interest, although it is clear that Forrest's conduct is unethical because it is dishonest.

The following vignette raises somewhat different issues:

> Raoul provides parenting assessments of clients for his agency. Some of his coworkers think he is unsympathetic to clients because he has never had children.

Raoul's job requires decisionmaking in the service of others (Element 1), but there is no interest that interferes with his objectivity in making those decisions (Element 2). As a result, this situation does not present a conflict of interest. There may be an ethical problem if Raoul makes poor decisions because of biases that affect his judgment. If so, this would be an issue of competence rather than one of conflict of interest.

In the following case example, both elements are present and a conflict of interest exists:

> John and Fred are on the board of directors of the Abba Foster Care Agency. John is the husband and Fred is the uncle of Susan, the executive director and founder of Abba. They have helped her build the agency through board participation since the agency was established 10 years ago. Building Abba has been Susan's lifelong dream.

As board members, John and Fred are in decisionmaking positions that affect others (Element 1). Indeed, one of the primary responsibilities of the board is to hire, evaluate, and, when necessary, dismiss the executive director. John and Fred have an interest (their relationships with Susan) that could affect their objectivity in making decisions concerning the Abba agency (Element 2). Both elements are present, and John and Fred have a conflict of interest.

Each of the two elements presents important issues that child welfare professionals must consider when determining if there is a conflict of interest.

Element 1: Being Entrusted to Exercise Objective Judgment

The first consideration in determining whether a conflict of interest exists is the nature of an employee's duties. The key issue is whether an employee has decisionmaking authority that requires him to exercise objective judgment, that is, to make decisions guided by some level of expertise rather than by rules. The responsibility to exercise objective judgment may be based on expertise acquired through professional training. A person with an MSW, for example, may be entrusted to make decisions regarding case plans because of her professional qualifications. Individuals who merely follow rules do not usually exercise objective judgment based on expertise. Only individuals who are entrusted to make judgments requiring discretionary authority usually have the responsibility to use that authority in an objective manner. As a general rule of thumb, the more that a position involves responsibilities for making decisions or recommendations, the more likely it is that Element 1 (entrustment to exercise objective judgment) is present. Because decisionmaking is required of all child welfare professionals, from caseworkers to administrators, it is safe to assume that Element 1 applies to them.

The client, the agency, and the public are justified in trusting that the child welfare professional will make objective judgments that will be in the best interest of the children they serve. Because professionals exercise judgment on behalf of others, a conflict of interest that could compromise a professional's judgment places the client, the agency, and the public in a vulnerable position and creates an ethical problem. The following case illustrates the problem:

> Terrel is a caseworker. He would like to adopt Jason, one of the children for whom he has been assigned responsibility. Jason's current foster parents, however, have recently expressed an interest in adopting him. As part of the adoption procedure, Terrel will assess the foster parents as prospective adoptive parents for Jason.

Jason, Terrel's client, is justified in expecting that Terrel will make an objective judgment on the suitability of his foster parents to serve as his adoptive parents. Terrel's interest in adopting, however, makes his judgment less reliable than it would be otherwise. The result may be that poor decisionmaking will take place regarding Jason's future. The ethical problem of Terrel's conflict of interest also extends to his relationship with his employer, because the agency entrusts Terrel to make objective judgments in the best interests of the children that the agency serves. Should this situation result in public questions about the objectivity of child welfare professionals, public trust in the agency may be undermined.

The first element of a conflict of interest is that the professional makes judgments in the service of another party. Positions in which the professional's duties require discretionary decisionmaking and where conflicts of interest may arise include caseworker, supervisor, and manager positions (as opposed, for example, to such positions as receptionist, messenger, or word processor). In these positions, the client, the agency, and the public rely on the sound judgment of the professional.

Element 2: Interests that Interfere with Objectivity

The second element of a conflict of interest is that the individual has an interest that could interfere with the exercise of objective judgment in his or her professional capacity. The term "interest" should be broadly construed to refer to any obligation, loyalty, responsibility, duty or desire. A professional's primary obligation is to act in her client's best interest and serve her agency. A conflict of interest may arise when the professional has another interest that, from the viewpoint of a reasonable person, could render her professional judgment less reliable than it would otherwise be, thereby compromising how she carries out her professional duties.

Not every interest gives rise to a conflict of interest. A caseworker, for example, may aspire to become a supervisor. Although this interest may affect his work, it is unlikely to interfere with his professional judgment in planning for and serving his clients. At the same time, the relevant issue is not how the professional assesses his or her ability to exercise objective judgment in the face of a particular interest, but the presence of the interest itself. An agency's day care licensing representative, for example, may believe that she can objectively evaluate the day care center that her own children attend. Her employer, however, could justifiably be concerned that her judgments about the day care center are less reliable than they would be otherwise. The day care center likewise may be concerned about the objectivity of her assessment regarding their licensing status.

As these examples illustrate, interests that cause a conflict may be personal factors that affect obligations to clients and to the agency simultaneously. A conflict of interest also may occur between the best interest of the client and the interests of the agency. The following case illustrates such a situation:

> The state child welfare agency contracts with the XYZ Agency to provide case management services. XYZ understands that it is in the children's best interest to expedite permanency planning so that they can leave foster care as soon as possible. The longer that children remain in foster care, however, the more XYZ is paid under the contract.

In this situation, a conflict exists between the agency's interest (greater financial rewards if children remain in foster care longer) and the best interest of children (permanent placements as soon as possible).

ACTUAL, POTENTIAL, AND APPARENT CONFLICTS

Conflicts of interest may be actual, potential, or apparent. An actual conflict of interest occurs when a professional entrusted to exercise objective judgement in the service of an agency and its clients has an interest that could interfere with the objectivity of that judgment. An actual conflict of interest does not require that the professional act on his or her interest; it merely requires that the interest exists. An example of an actual conflict of interest is the following:

> Sue, a licensing representative, owns an interest in a new agency, the Alpha Agency, which is applying for a license. Sue has been assigned to review the Alpha application.

An actual conflict of interest causes an ethical problem because individuals who depend on the sound judgment of the professional are vulnerable to poor decisionmaking regarding their welfare. One way to prevent this ethical dilemma is to recognize a conflict before it is actual (that is, when it is a potential conflict) and take steps to avoid it.

A potential conflict of interest exists when there is no existing conflict, but there is some likelihood that a situation will change and the professional will have an interest that could reasonably affect decisionmaking in the future. In Sue's case, a potential conflict of interest would be presented if the facts were slightly altered:

> Sue, a licensing representative, owns an interest in the Alpha Agency. Alpha is considering applying for a license but has not yet done so.

When the situation is reconstructed in this way, there is a potential conflict of interest. There is some likelihood that Alpha will apply for a license and some likelihood that Sue would be asked to determine whether the agency should be licensed. When the situation is identified as a potential conflict, Sue can prevent an actual conflict (as discussed later in this chapter).

Apparent conflicts of interest also arise when, although there is not a potential or actual conflict, an individual who is unaware of the facts of the situation may reasonably infer that a conflict exists. Child welfare professionals must be watchful for apparent conflicts of interest because they may undermine the confidence of clients or the trust of the public. Apparent conflicts of interest may, in fact, undermine confidence and trust as much as actual conflicts of interest. As an example, if Sue in the previous examples did not have responsibilities regarding licensing but instead held a senior administrative position at the public agency to which the Alpha Agency is applying for a license, an observer could reasonably infer that she may influence the licensing process.

DETERMINING IF A CONFLICT OF INTEREST EXISTS

A decision tree such as the one in Figure 5-1 may be used to determine if there is a conflict of interest.

Figure 5-1. Decision Tree

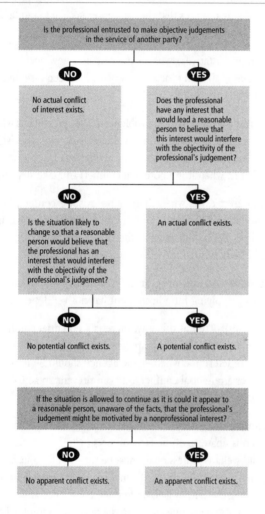

TYPES OF CONFLICTS OF INTEREST

Conflicts of interest generally involve the existence of an interest that makes a professional's judgment less reliable or objective than it would be otherwise. Conflicts of interest fall into two different categories: those involving private interests and those involving multiple relationships.

Private Interests

Different types of private interests may contribute to a conflict of interest. Some private interests may be financial, as in the following example:

> Kathy sells cosmetics in her off-hours. During client visits, she offers her products to female clients.

Kathy has an actual conflict of interest because she has an interest that would lead a reasonable person to conclude that she favors clients who purchase her products over those who do not. A conflict of interest exists even if Kathy does not favor customers over noncustomers. Kathy also is abusing her power. Because she has a more powerful position in the professional-client relationship, her clients may feel pressured to purchase products that they do not want or need. This issue is discussed more fully later in this chapter.

Multiple Relationships

A second type of conflict of interest involves multiple relationships (sometimes called a dual relationships). When a child welfare professional has a nonprofessional relationship with an individual for whom he is also expected to make professional decisions, he is involved in a multiple relationship. The professional has both a professional and a nonprofessional relationship with the same person. One common situation in which multiple relationships give rise to a conflict of interest occurs when two coworkers have a relationship outside of the office. The following example illustrates this type of situation:

> Tina is a caseworker in a large agency and has been dating another caseworker, Jeff. Recently, Tina was promoted to supervisor over Jeff and other caseworkers.

The conflict of interest arises in this case because Tina is now in a position to make decisions regarding Jeff's work and her decisionmaking could be influenced by her personal interest in him. Multiple relationships also may arise between professionals and clients, as in the following example:

> Ron, a caseworker, lives in a small town. He has just been assigned responsibility for working with and developing a service plan for a family whom he knows well through his church.

Ron has a multiple relationship with the family because he now has professional responsibilities for them and already has a nonprofessional relationship.

Finally, a professional relationship with a client can become a personal relationship and cause a conflict of interest, as in the following example:

> Teri is very fond of her client, Claire, and says that Claire is "a lot of fun." Because of her affection for Claire, Teri has overlooked several of Claire's violations of agency rules and has failed to recognize that Claire is currently abusing drugs.

Teri's judgment has been affected by her personal feelings for Claire, a situation that illustrates the risks associated with having nonprofessional relationships with clients.

The Illinois *Code of Ethics for Child Welfare Professionals* addresses conflicts of interest that arise from private interests and multiple relationships. It provides the following with regard to private interests:

> Child welfare professionals should not allow their private interests, whether personal, financial, or of any other sort, to conflict or appear to conflict with their professional duties and responsibilities. Any conduct that would lead a reasonable person to conclude that the child welfare professional might be biased or motivated by personal gain or private interest in the performance of duties should be avoided.

> Child welfare professionals should avoid professional matters where they have private financial or personal interest. If a situation arises where such a conflict may exist, child welfare professionals should consult with an appropriate superior and take steps to eliminate any potential or real conflict.

The Illinois *Code* provides the following regarding multiple relationships:

> Child welfare professionals should take into consideration the potential harm that intimate, social, or other nonprofessional contact and relationships with clients, family members, foster parents, colleagues, and supervisors could have on those with whom they have professional relationships and on their professional objective judgment and performance.

> Child welfare professionals should avoid any conduct that would lead a reasonable person to conclude that the child welfare professional might be biased or motivated by personal interest in the performance of duties.

Whenever feasible, child welfare professionals should avoid professional relationships when a preexisting nonprofessional relationship is present. Child welfare professionals should discuss past, existing, and potential multiple relationships with their appropriate superiors and resolve them in a manner which avoids harming and/or exploiting affected persons.

Child welfare professionals who are also foster parents should disclose and have ongoing discussions regarding these dual roles with their appropriate superior in order to prevent conflicts of interest, abuse of power, or the suggestion of impropriety in carrying out professional activities.

ADDRESSING CONFLICTS OF INTEREST

There are three ways to address conflicts of interest: disclosure of the interest, recusal, and divestment or change of position. Each of these approaches will be appropriate under certain circumstances and inappropriate under others.

Disclosing Interest

Sometimes, a conflict of interest may become ethically acceptable if the individual who has the conflict discloses the interest to his client or his employer. Disclosing the interest does not resolve a conflict. The conflict remains, but with the disclosure of the interest, the client or the employer can choose to dissolve or maintain the relationship. If a client or an employer has full knowledge of the conflict, accepts that a conflict exists, and chooses to continue the relationship, the ethical dilemma may be adequately resolved.

A disclosure of interest in the child welfare setting, however, is usually not an adequate solution to conflicts of interest for two reasons. First, it may be impossible or impractical for the professional to disclose the interest to the party for whom she makes judgments. The director of a public agency, for example, is entrusted by society to make judgments in the best interest of the children served by the agency. If this professional finds herself in a conflict of interest, to whom would she disclose that interest—to the children the agency serves, their families, or the community? Such disclosures are not practiceable. In addition, even if the interest could be disclosed, there would be difficulties obtaining consensus about the acceptability of the conflict.

Second, a disclosure of interest is not an adequate solution in child welfare settings because clients typically are not in a position to choose to dissolve or maintain their relationships with the child welfare professional. Disclosure as an approach to resolving a conflict of interest assumes that the client has freely sought out the service of the professional and is capable of altering the relationship if he determines that the conflict adversely affects him. In child welfare settings, courts usually mandate that clients participate in services. If an interest is disclosed to a client, he or she will not have the freedom to choose to dissolve the relationship. Another problem with this approach is that clients in child welfare often are children who may not be able to understand the nature of the conflict and who cannot decide whether the conflict would interfere with the caseworker's judgment in their best interest.

Because of the limitations on disclosure as a means of resolving conflicts of interest in child welfare, the professional has an obligation to refrain, as much as possible, from making judgments in conflict of interest situations. This obligation applies even when a client finds a particular conflict of interest acceptable. If, for example, a client does not find it objectionable that his therapist enjoys playing golf with him (a multiple relationship situation), the therapist nonetheless has a professional obligation to avoid such a personal relationship.

Recusal

Recusal is perhaps the most common strategy for defusing conflicts of interest. The person with the conflict withdraws from the decisionmaking process when the conflict situation occurs. This approach is most effective when the conflict is not an ongoing situation and other staff members are available to undertake the additional responsibility. The following example illustrates the use of recusal:

> Alice is a therapist for the Beta Agency and also has a part-time job as a social worker in a hospital in a neighboring town. On occasion, children who are her clients at the Beta agency are brought to the hospital, and a hospital social worker is asked to consult with the child and foster family. Because Alice recognizes this situation as a potential conflict of interest, she recuses herself by asking that children referred from the Beta Agency be assigned to other hospital social workers.

In this situation, Alice avoids a potential conflict between her obligation to the Beta Agency and her obligation to the hospital by recusing herself from consultations with children referred to the hospital from her agency. When the likelihood of a conflict of interest is high, a child welfare professional should consider submitting a letter to her employer that explains the potential conflict of interest and proposes a way to recuse herself so that a conflict can be avoided. Alice, for example, might write the following letter:

Joan Smith
Executive Director, Beta Agency

Dear Ms. Smith,

I have been a therapist with the Beta Agency for three years and have recently
accepted a part-time social work position at St. Joseph's Hospital. Because some
of the agency's children and families are referred to St. Joseph's, there is a potential conflict of interest. My supervisor at St. Joseph's has given me permission to
transfer all cases involving Beta clients to other social workers on the hospital
staff. Please let me know if this plan sufficiently addresses the potential conflict
of interest.

Sincerely,
Alice Johnson, LCSW

cc: Personnel

This type of communication fully discloses potential conflicts to a professional's
employer and proposes a strategy to avoid a conflict of interest situation. The employer may determine that the conflict cannot be handled in the proposed manner. In
Alice's case, for example, her supervisor may not accept the transfer plan because there
are too few available social workers to accept transfers of all the cases from Beta or
such conflicts occur so frequently that recusal is not practical. Nonetheless, recusals
often are sufficient to address conflicts of interest, particularly if they are intermittent.

Divestment or Change of Position

When a conflict is ongoing, it is unlikely that recusal will sufficiently address the conflict. The only solution may be for the professional to divest, that is, dispose of the outside interest. The following example illustrates divestment:

> Chan is a senior administrator at the Gamma Residential Care Facility.
> He also owns stock in the Feta Food Service Company. The manage-
> ment at Gamma is considering contracting with Feta for daily meal
> service for their residents. Chan recognizes a contract with Feta would
> be a conflict of interest and decides to sell his stock in Feta.

Because the conflict would be ongoing in Chan's case, it could not be addressed by disclosure or recusal. As a result, Chan chose to resolve the conflict by divesting himself
of his ownership interest in Feta. Another means by which a professional may resolve
a conflict is to leave one's position, as illustrated by the following example:

> Fred is a supervisor at the Chi Agency. He is married to Sally, a thera-
> pist at the Delphi Agency. Chi and Delphi are small agencies in the
> process of merging. Following the reorganization, Sally is assigned to

work in Fred's department under his supervision. Recognizing the potential conflict of interest, Sally decides to resign from Delphi and move to the Eta Agency.

As in the previous case, the conflict facing Sally would be ongoing. Because Fred and Sally do not want to dispose of their interest (their marriage), the only means of resolving the conflict may be that either Sally or Fred resign.

THE CASE OF GIFTS

One of the most common and confusing issues related to conflicts of interest involves gifts. A gift often creates an apparent conflict because it gives the appearance that the recipient may be motivated to favor the individual who gave the gift. The following example illustrates the difficulties posed by gifts:

> Gabi is a caseworker for a private agency. Her clients, Robbie and Sammy, have been with their foster family, the Chodzcos, for three years, and the Chodzcos want to adopt the boys. Parental rights recently were terminated, and Gabi testified in favor of termination. After the decision was made, the Chodzcos gave Gabi a $250 gift certificate to a local department store.

This type of situation can be handled effectively by expressing gratitude for the sentiment behind the gift, but tactfully explaining that it cannot be accepted. When a gift can be returned, the professional should return it. When it is not possible or practical to return a gift (such as a floral arrangement), the professional should offer to donate the gift to another party in the name of the person who gave the gift. In all cases, professionals should be familiar with their agencies' rules regarding the receipt of gifts.

UNRESOLVABLE CONFLICTS

In certain situations, a conflict of interest cannot be resolved. The very context of the work situation may entail a conflict, as in the example of the XYZ Agency. The contract with the agency provides for reimbursement that is based on the length of time children are in foster care. Because of this reimbursement formula, XYZ has a financial incentive to delay children's discharge from foster care despite the fact that it is in the best interest of children to achieve permanency as soon as possible. An additional conflict may arise in the XYZ Agency example because the cases of children who have been in foster care longer may require less work than new cases referred to the agency, and caseworkers may have an incentive to retain older cases so that they can avoid having to take newer, more demanding cases.

In situations in which conflicts of interest cannot be resolved, professionals and agencies must rely on their personal integrity and refer to their professional code of ethics to ensure that children's best interests remain primary. In the XYZ Agency example, efforts might be made to change the reimbursement formula and case assignment policies. If these practices are not or cannot be changed, constant efforts should be made to ensure that financial and logistical pressures are subordinated to the best interests of each child.

ABUSE OF POWER

There is a risk that a conflict of interest will escalate into an abuse of power. An abuse of power occurs when a professional uses his or her position for personal gain. The following example illustrates how an abuse of power may occur when a professional finds himself in a conflict of interest situation:

> Carl is a program director in a child welfare agency and also serves as a foster parent for the same agency. He is interested in adopting a child for whom he is currently caring, and he also wants to adopt her sibling who is currently placed with a different foster family. Because of his position as a program director with the agency, he obtains the confidential personal history of the other foster parent and the address of the birthfamily. He visits the birthfamily and urges them to ask their caseworker to place both children together in his home.

Carl has a multiple relationship conflict of interest. He works at the agency that licensed him as a foster parent. He abused his power by obtaining records that were only available to him because of his position, thereby violating the confidentiality of the foster family and the birthfamily. He further abused his power by visiting the birthfamily and trying to influence them to do something that was in his best interests, but not necessarily theirs.

Abuses of power create a particularly serious ethical problem because they represent a breach of fiduciary duty by the professional. The state gives child welfare professionals access to information, power over vulnerable people, and discretionary judgment about the use of resources with the implicit understanding that this power will be used responsibly and only for official purposes. Because of the imbalance of power between the professional and the families who are involved in the system involuntarily, it is particularly important for the professional to be scrupulously careful when using her official authority. Misuse of official authority is also very troubling because it can undermine public confidence in the integrity of the system if it is exposed.

Carl clearly abused his power in this case because he had access to confidential information in the family's file only as a result of his official position, yet he used that information for his own personal purposes. Likewise, in visiting the foster family and pressuring them to talk to their caseworker, he used his official authority to further his own nonprofessional ends. Another common context for the abuse of power is decision-making about the allocation of agency resource. For instance, a child welfare professional who awards contracts or licenses on the basis of his personal connections rather than on objective criteria abuses his power. Indeed, because the danger of abuse of power often creates the appearance of a conflict of interest, child welfare professionals should generally recuse themselves from decisions in which they have a significant personal interest.

Summary

A conflict of interest occurs when a child welfare professional, entrusted to exercise objective judgment in the service of an agency and its clients, has an interest (either a private interest or a multiple relationship) that could interfere with the objectivity of that judgment. Conflicts of interest pose problems because they interfere with a professional's objective judgment and can undermine a client's trust, compromise services to clients, and/or jeopardize the credibility of the professional's agency. Conflicts of interest can be actual, potential, or apparent.

There are ways to make conflicts of interest less problematic. Although acceptable in other professions, disclosure of the interest is not often an effective strategy in child welfare settings. When the conflict is only periodic, a professional can recuse herself when a conflict occurs. When a conflict is ongoing, however, a professional may have to divest herself of the outside interest or leave her position.

Occasionally, conflicts are unresolvable because of existing policies. In such cases, child welfare professionals should try to avoid the interference of any interest with their judgment. In all cases, professionals should be aware of the potential for an abuse of power in conflict of interest situations and should ensure that such occurrences are avoided.

CASE STUDIES FOR CHAPTER 5

Case Study 5-1. George is a regional administrator for the public child welfare agency and has been asked to join an advisory board for an organization that operates a number of day care facilities. He will not be paid for his service. The organization has a contract with the public child welfare agency. Although the agency's conflict of interest rule does not categorically prohibit advisory board service by employees, it prohibits such service when it creates a conflict of interest. In his role at the agency, George does not have any decisionmaking authority over day care licensing and contracts. Would George have a conflict of interest if he agreed to sit on the advisory board?

Case Study 5-2. Heidi is a case manager for the Beta Foster Care Agency. Her sister Francine is a secretary in a law firm that is suing Beta. Francine handles documents for the case, and on occasion, she shares information with Heidi. Does Heidi have a conflict of interest?

Case Study 5-3. Bartholomew is a caseworker who is known in his unit as being very logical and fair. By chance, a distant cousin of Bartholomew is assigned to Bartholomew's caseload. Does Bartholomew have a conflict of interest?

Case Study 5-4. Mandy is a child welfare caseworker. Several of Mandy's clients live near and shop in a grocery store owned by her family. Does Mandy have a conflict of interest?

Case Study 5-5. Freida represents the public child welfare agency in a service providers' networking group. Most of the service providers receive funding from the public agency. The group plans to hire a coordinator. At each meeting, Freida advocates that the group hire her friend, Theresa, for the position. Does Freida have a multiple relationship conflict of interest?

Case Study 5-6. Sina has built a good rapport with Tommy. She has been his caseworker for three years, and she has been very responsive to and supportive of him. Tommy is now 12. One day he calls Sina and asks, "Can't you adopt me?" Does Sina have conflict of interest?

Case Study 5-7. When Martha was a caseworker with the health department, Marie was her client. Martha transferred to the public child welfare agency, and Marie was assigned to her caseload. Does Martha have a conflict of interest?

Case Study 5-8. Jeremy, a caseworker, has worked very hard to gain Jewel's trust. He wants to support her so that she can regain custody of her 2-year-old son, BJ.

Over the last two months, Jewel has made serious attempts to overcome her heroin addiction. The 12-month permanency deadline has arrived, and Jeremy is not certain whether he should advocate for Jewel or concede that it will still take a significant amount of time for her to recover and provide a safe home for BJ. What kind of conflict does Jeremy have?

Case Study 5-9. Jim has been looking for a part-time job to supplement his income as a caseworker for the public child welfare agency. Because Jim is an ordained minister, he applies for a part-time pastoral counseling position at Alpha Clinic, a local drug rehabilitation center. Jim knows that his current employer has a contract with Alpha Clinic, and he worries that there may be a conflict of interest. He consults his supervisor and learns that quite a few of the agency's clients are referred to the drug rehabilitation program at Alpha. Would Jim have an actual, potential, or apparent conflict of interest if he accepts the counseling position at the rehabilitation center? If so, how could it be resolved?

Chapter 6

Competence

Competence has to do with the quality of service that a professional provides to clients. Because child welfare professionals have decisionmaking power over the lives of their clients, they must be conscientious about their ability to offer clients the greatest opportunity to improve their situations. Child welfare professionals must have sufficient knowledge and skills to perform the tasks assigned to them, and once they master initial tasks, they must continually update their knowledge and abilities. Child welfare professionals should never misrepresent their qualifications when applying for a position at any child welfare agency. This chapter discusses the meaning of competence, examines the relationship between competence and accountability, and offers recommendations for enhancing competence.

COMPETENCE AS A KEY VALUE

One of the key values of ethical child welfare practice is that the professional is competent to perform the tasks for which he or she is responsible. Competence means that the professional has the requisite ability to carry out his or her professional responsibilities. The Illinois *Code of Ethics for Child Welfare Professionals* outlines the obligations related to professional competence as follows:

> Child welfare professionals should provide services only within the boundaries of their competence based on their education, training, supervised experience, and professional experience.

> Child welfare professionals should accurately represent their qualifications, educational backgrounds, and professional credentials.

> Child welfare professionals should be aware of current professional information and take advantage of continuing professional education in order to maintain a high level of competence.

Professionals receive preparation for their work from formal education, on-the-job training, supervision, and working closely with a more experienced professional.

Having appropriate credentials, training, and experience, however, does not automatically mean that the professional will achieve the best outcomes for her clients. Professionals must be aware of the limits of their knowledge and must be attuned to situations that are new to them or to the field or that present issues for which there is little research or data to inform decisions. In such cases, professionals must be particularly careful to consult supervisors, clinical consultants, and other professionals; read relevant articles; and think through decisions cautiously. The *Code of Ethics* of the National Association of Social Workers states:

When generally recognized standards do not exist with respect to an emerging area of practice, social workers should exercise careful judgment and take responsible steps — including appropriate education, training, consultation and supervision to ensure the competence of their work and protect clients from harm.

Agency administrators also have ethical responsibilities to ensure that services to clients are competent. Administrators should fulfill this duty by ensuring that child welfare professionals are qualified to serve children and families and that they receive quality, ongoing on-the-job training. Administrators also should encourage continuing education for professionals and be aware of current information in the field, particularly evidence-based information about the effectiveness of programs and services.

Issues related to professional competence are raised in the following example:

> Jill is 21 and has never worked in social services. After graduating from college with a degree in liberal arts, she seeks a position with the public child welfare agency because she wants to help people. Jill has a very strong belief that clients served by the child welfare system have been oppressed and that all they need is someone to believe in them and treat them nicely. She thinks that other caseworkers are cynical, do not have compassion for their clients, and are judgmental. Jill's first client is Marge, a heroin addict. Marge tells Jill that her placement at a drug treatment program is "terrible" and that other patients stole all of her money. Marge asks Jill for $30 so that she will have money through the end of the month. Jill's heart goes out to Marge, and she gives her the money.

Jill is clearly kind-hearted, and her generosity can help her become an extremely effective child welfare professional in the future. In her interaction with Marge, however, she demonstrated a lack of competence. She is unfamiliar with the dynamics of substance abuse and with agency regulations forbidding staff to provide clients with personal funds. The most serious problem, however, is not that Jill may have made a mistake in allowing Marge to take advantage of her and may have contributed to Marge's addiction. It is that Jill relied on her personal judgment and did not collaborate with more experienced colleagues. It is likely that Jill's supervisor will ask her about the interaction with Marge, and Jill would be well served to honestly discuss the situation with her.

Competence and the Related Concept of Accountability

Accountability and competence are closely related. Accountability requires that a professional offer services that are most likely to help the client achieve desired outcomes, evaluate client progress on an ongoing basis using valid measures, and share the results with the client. In the child welfare profession, accountability also includes a duty to the court and society to use strategies that are most likely to result in the protection of children, and whenever possible, the preservation of their families.

Accountability requires that a child welfare professional accurately estimate the degree to which their knowledge and skills match what is needed to help the client, consult with supervisors if they believe that there is a mismatch, and use their best efforts to ensure that clients receive services with an objective record of success. Some social workers view accountability in terms of respect for clients, a commitment to the client's best interests, and encouraging client self-determination. Although these goals are worthy, they are vague and permit considerable leeway in actions and outcomes, some of which may not be in the beneficial to the client. Evidence-based practice (the conscientious, explicit, and judicious use of current best evidence in making decisions about the care of individuals) is a more dependable route to successful outcomes.

Professionals may overestimate their competence to provide certain kinds of services and may underestimate the specific knowledge and skills that may be available from other sources. Because clients (and the public) rarely know when a child welfare worker is not adequately trained or supervised, accountability can be ensured only when professionals know themselves and admit their limitations.

Competence in Assessment, Intervention, and Evaluation

Professional competence is critical to a successful outcome in three contexts: assessment of the client's needs and the available strategies to meet those needs, implementation of the selected intervention, and evaluation of the results of the intervention.

Competence in Assessment

Assessment requires a number of decisions: the type of data that is needed about the client's problems and the potential for problem resolution; the processes for collection of data (such as by self-reports or through observation); and the integration of data into a manageable plan. Some child welfare professionals have been trained in a specific practice or theoretical framework that they use to assess client's needs. A professional trained in psychology, for example, may be inclined to assess each client in terms of his or her pathologies. This approach, however, may not be appropriate in each case. For example, a client with disturbing behaviors may have experienced successes due to compensating strengths and outside resources, and these aspects should be explored.

Sources of assessment data. Irrespective of the practice or theoretical framework that a professional uses, data may be collected in only a limited number of ways. Specifically, data can be collected through self-reporting (oral or written reports from clients or family members), self-monitoring (in which clients track specific behaviors or events in their lives); observation in role-play or real life; and physiological measures. Case records contain information based on one or more of these sources.

Each method of data collection has advantages and disadvantages. Professionals should critically appraise the accuracy and completeness of different kinds of data. If, for example, a parent reports that she is a good mother and knows how to use positive methods to discipline her child, the professional should determine how best to verify these statements. Judging the accuracy of sources of data may require skills in discovering related research findings, such as through computer online databases. Administrators should ensure that professionals have access to such tools and to summaries of up-to-date research on the important practice decisions that professionals are called upon to make.

Integrating information from different sources. Child welfare professionals deal with complex problems that require the integration of information from diverse sources. The process involves reviewing all the information gathered about a client to assess the problem and potential solutions. This process can be overwhelming, and certain errors may occur. One common error is confirmation bias, that is, looking only for information that supports preferred views and ignoring counter-evidence. Another error is disregard of statistical data regarding clients' problems and solutions and reliance instead on clinical intuition. It is particularly important at the integration stage of assessment that the professional discuss her thinking with supervisors and colleagues who can assist her in identifying biases or lapses in integrating important facts.

Selecting service methods. A child welfare professional often must make decisions about the service methods to use, the level of services to offer (such as 5 or 10 sessions of parent training), the provider of the service, and the methods of tracking and measuring progress. Accountability to clients, the courts, and the public requires that service methods be selected that are acceptable to clients and that the methods will likely result in positive outcomes in an efficient manner with minimum negative effects.

Administrators have an obligation to collect data on the effectiveness of the service methods that are recommended for clients. Professionals should rely on supervisors and on research data for assistance in determining whether a particular service will help address a client's need and whether another service would yield greater benefits.

Competence in Intervention

Once a decision has been made about the appropriate service for the client, implementation is the next step. Although this phase of the professional's relationship with the client may appear to require less in terms of decisionmaking, it may in fact involve a number of key decisions. How a service is provided can influence its outcomes. Procedural fidelity refers to the match between how a service should be implemented for maximal effect and how it is actually implemented. An intervention is sometimes less effective than planned because of the dilution effect. The dilution effect occurs when a service is not delivered as intended in "full strength" form because of time constraints, limited resources, lack of client cooperation, or limited staff training. Examples of the dilution effect include a reduction in the number of weeks recommended for attendance at a drug rehabilitation program or the use of a relatively untrained provider to deliver a service that has been found to be effective with trained personnel.

Competence in Evaluating Outcomes

The third component of accountability concerns the evaluation of the outcomes of the interventions. Clients, the courts, and society have a right to know whether child welfare interventions help, harm, or are irrelevant. Agency administrators play an important role in providing professionals with relevant, feasible ways to measure clients' improvement or lack of improvement as services are provided. Ongoing monitoring allows for timely case management decisions and the provision of information to the client about adjustments to the case plan. When the client is making progress, service methods that seem to contribute to positive outcomes can be continued; when progress is nil or outcomes decrease in positive value, these developments can be detected at an early point and decisions made about next steps.

Careful recording of successes and failures with clients also assists the agency in providing a complete assessment to the public of its track record in solving the problems of the children and families that the agency serves. The actions of a child welfare agency must have social validity; that is, the agency's goals, methods, and the unintended or unforeseen effects of its interventions must be acceptable to the community as a whole.

COMPETENCE AND RECORDKEEPING

Recordkeeping is critically important to the competent provision of social services. Careful documentation in complete case records assists professionals to assess progress with clients as services are provided. Complete records ensure that other professionals who are involved in serving the client have a full understanding of the client's situation. Good recordkeeping is particularly important in cases of transfer of responsibility for a client from one caseworker to another in the agency or from one agency to another. Finally, quality recordkeeping also keeps the courts, clients, and society adequately informed about the successes and failures of the child welfare system. The Illinois *Code of Ethics for Child Welfare Professionals* states that:

> Child welfare professionals should accurately and truthfully document their professional work according to agency policy and/or legal requirements in order to ensure accountability and continuity in the provision of services to clients.

A case record should include the following information:

- A complete social history, assessment, and treatment plan that states the client's problems, his or her reason for requesting or needing services, objectives and a relevant timetable for achieving the objectives, intervention strategy, planned number and duration of contacts, methods for assessment and evaluation of progress, plan to end services, and reasons for ending services.

- Procedures used to obtain consent for the release of information and signed consent forms for release of information and treatment.

- Notes on all contacts made with third parties (such as family members, acquaintances, and other professionals), whether the contacts were made in person or by telephone, a brief description of the contacts and any important events surrounding them.

- Notes on any consultations with other professionals, including the date the client was referred to other professionals for services.

- A brief description of the social worker's reasons for all decisions made and interventions provided during the course of services.

- Any instructions, recommendations, and advice provided to the client, including referrals and suggestions to seek consultation from specialists (including physicians).

- A description of all contacts with clients, including the type of contact (in person or via telephone or in individual, family, couples, or group counseling), and dates and times of the contacts.

- Notations regarding any failed or canceled appointments.

- Summaries of previous or current psychological, psychiatric, or medical evaluations relevant to the social worker's intervention.

- Reasons for termination of services and final assessment.

- Copies of all relevant documents, such as correspondence, fee agreements, and court documents.

- Information summarizing any critical incidents (such as suicide attempts, threats made by the client toward third parties, child abuse, or family crises) and the social worker's response.

(Reamer, 1998)

LIMITS ON COMPETENCE

Several factors may limit competence: faulty attitudes ("I already know everything I need to know"); faulty ethical judgments (whether intentional or inadvertent); lack of specialized knowledge (such as an inadequate understanding of the issues involved in sexual abuse or mental illness); lack of updated knowledge ("I haven't worked in the field for 10 years since I obtained my degree"); or personal impairment (such as illness, substance abuse problems, or an impossible workload). The following example raises issues related to professional competence:

Tito, a child protective services investigator, believes that school social workers over-report abuse and neglect. In one case, Tito is called to investigate a possible case of sexual abuse after a school social worker reports that a child has stated that her mother's boyfriend was molesting her. When Tito interviews the child, Patty, she will not look at Tito and she denies the allegation, although in a tentative way. Patty's mother vehemently denies the allegation and states that the boyfriend is out of town on business. The school social worker states that Patty has a best friend in whom she confides. Tito, however, decides, based on Patty's denial of the allegation, that she has probably made up the story to get attention and that the social worker inferred too much from what

Patty said. He decides that he has done enough work on the case; he
does not take the time to seek out Patty's friend; and he makes the determination that the report is unfounded.

Tito began his investigation with a bias against incidents reported by school social
workers. As a result of his bias, he did not conduct a thorough investigation. He may
have too eagerly determined the report to be unfounded. Tito's assumption may be
correct, and it may be that he properly determined the report to be unfounded.
Nevertheless, there was more that Tito could have done to ensure that he had all the
information he needed, such as interviewing Patty's friend and the mother's boyfriend.

MISREPRESENTING COMPETENCE

Professionals can misrepresent their competence in a number of ways. Some misrepresentations are slight, and some are blatantly fraudulent. In either situation, the professional is deceiving others. Because clients, agencies, and society trust professionals
to use their expertise to provide effective services, misrepresentation of competence
raises a real risk of harm for all concerned. In addition to the parties who rely on professionals and trust them, the individual himself can be harmed by misrepresentations
of competence, including the possibility of losing his job should the misrepresentation
be discovered.

Sometimes professionals may represent themselves as being competent in a particular
area when their training is in a very different area of specialization. An example is a
professional who represents expertise in child welfare but who has an advanced degree
in a subject unrelated to child welfare. Another example is the professional who has an
advanced degree from an unaccredited school. The following example illustrates a situation in which a professional's training may not be in accord with accepted professional training:

> Franz applies for a therapist position with a child welfare agency. He has
> a Ph.D. that he obtained in 10 months from an unaccredited school in
> spiritual counseling. Franz considers himself a biblical fundamentalist,
> and he focuses his counseling on the salvation potential of individuals
> who have sinned. On his job application, Franz does not disclose how
> his training differs from traditional social work preparation.

On rare occasions, individuals intentionally lie about their credentials in order to
obtain a more lucrative position or achieve more status in an agency. In this case, Franz
has misrepresented his credentials through omitting key information about the nature
of his degree or its orientation. Franz's degree is not from an accredited school of

social work, counseling, or psychology and is based on religious beliefs rather than practice-related research findings. Had Franz disclosed this information to the agency, the administrators may well have determined that it is not appropriate for Franz to provide counseling for the agency's clients.

ENHANCING COMPETENCE

A professional has ongoing opportunities to enhance her skills throughout her career. A professional needs courage and a sincere interest in helping clients to candidly consider the match between her values, knowledge, and skills and what is needed to assist clients and avoid harming them. This review can assist professionals to identify the learning opportunities they need to enhance their competencies. Professionals should ask themselves the following questions:

What skills would I like to acquire?

What value would these skills have for my clients?

What exactly would I do (and not do) if I had this skill?

What steps take me closer to my goal?

What criteria would most accurately reflect mastery of skills?

Is this skill of value in other situations?

What training programs would be most effective in helping me learn this skill?

Ongoing evaluation of progress with clients provides a valuable source of feedback. Professionals should seek support from colleagues and supervisors as they strive to build the knowledge, skills, and outcomes that contribute to success. If such support is not possible in the professional's own agency, she should identify other professionals who share her values and goals and form a support or consultation group.

SUMMARY

Child welfare professionals should be competent, that is, they should have the requisite ability to perform their work-related tasks and carry out their professional responsibilities. Accountability is related to competence and requires that professionals not attempt to perform tasks or make judgments that fall outside their training, experience, or authority. Competence is relevant in assessment, intervention, and evaluation. In the area of assessment, competent child welfare professionals take into account the practice or theoretical framework in which they were trained, the sources of assessment data, and the service methods that are available. In the area of intervention, competent child welfare professionals maintain procedural fidelity so that clients receive services that will be most effective, and they resist the temptation to dilute services. In the area of evaluation, competent child welfare professionals document outcomes and evaluate results honestly and carefully. Competent interventions require diligent recordkeeping on the part of the professionals currently providing services so that professionals who provide services in the future fully understand clients' situations.

Several factors can affect the competence of individual professionals: biases, erroneous ethical judgments, lack of specialized or updated knowledge, and personal impairment. Professionals should monitor themselves to determine if any of these factors have affected their professional competence. At the same time, child welfare professionals should seek to enhance their competence throughout their careers.

CASE STUDIES FOR CHAPTER 6

Case Study 6-1. Giselle worked in a residential treatment facility for 15 years. She feels that her experience with troubled youth is so extensive that it is equivalent to an MSW. When she applies for a position with the public child welfare agency, she submits a resume that states that she has an MSW. Is there a problem with Giselle's actions?

Case Study 6-2. Carl is a caseworker. When he makes a home visit with his client, Maria, she complains that her son is losing weight. Carl tells Maria that there probably is no problem but that she should give him protein shakes. Is Carl competent to give this advice?

Case Study 6-3. Mark, a child protective services investigator, relies on self-reports of clients and significant others regarding the quality of parent-child interaction. In some cases, he speaks directly with the children. What questions are raised by his choice of information sources?

Case Study 6-4. Richard, a child welfare professional, relies on his intuition to integrate data about families in which abuse has been alleged. After 20 years in practice, he feels he has a "very good feel" for which types of parents abuse their children. What questions are raised by Richard's approach to the determination of child abuse?

Case Study 6-5. Frances, a child welfare caseworker, has been advised by her supervisor to refer a client to the XYZ Parenting Course. Frances has doubts about whether XYZ really helps parents improve their skills. What should she do?

Case Study 6-6. Mr. Zeno, a supervisor, tells his staff that the agency does not have the resources to provide parent training in the manner that has been effective in the past. He suggests cutting by half the number of training sessions offered. He believes that this approach will be just as effective. What ethical questions does this approach raise?

Case Study 6-7. Mrs. Rennert believes that with her current caseload, she is extremely overworked. A great deal of information that should be in the case records of her clients is not there. She attempts to justify her lack of recording by saying that she is simply protecting client confidentiality. What should the response be to her argument?

Case Study 6-8. Darleen has been a child welfare caseworker for 10 years. She feels quite irritated whenever training is required. She thinks that social work is plagued by fads that quickly pass and then become irrelevant. She feels confident that she does a good job with her clients, and she is not interested in new information. What issues are raised by Darleen's attitude?

Case Study 6-9. Pamela is a caseworker for a child welfare agency. She introduces herself as Dr. Pamela Jones. Pamela's doctorate is in art history. In fact, she has little formal social work training. May Pamela ethically refer to herself as "Dr. Jones"?

Chapter 7

Responsibilities to the Court

I mportant decisions concerning the well-being of children often are made in court-rooms. During a court hearing, the child welfare professional may be called upon to present information about a child or the child's family. The professional's testimony can have a significant impact on the decisions that a judge makes about a child. This chapter discusses court proceedings and the ethical duties of child welfare professionals when they testify in court: the responsibility to be fair, to be informed, and to be honest.

COURT PROCEEDINGS

All court proceedings are designed to resolve disputes between parties. In child welfare, there are different types of juvenile court proceedings regarding children and youth. Some proceedings are held to determine whether the state should take temporary custody of a child; other proceedings are held to determine the placement that is in the best interests of the child. An example of a court proceeding in child welfare is a hearing to resolve issues between a mother who feels that her children should be returned to her custody and the state, which takes the position that the mother has not adequately complied with services.

A number of individuals typically are involved in juvenile court proceedings, including:

Attorneys—Persons who represent parties before the court. Several attorneys are usually present at a child welfare proceeding and may include:

- The attorney for the state (sometimes known as the prosecutor)

- Defense counsel, who represents a party other than the state, often the child's caregiver

- Bar attorney (a title used in some states), who defends one party before the court when there are two defendants, and two defense attorneys are needed to prevent a conflict of interest.

- Guardian ad litem (GAL), who advocates for the best interests of the child independent of the parents and the state.

- An attorney representing the child welfare agency involved.

The Judge—The individual who listens to the evidence and arguments of the parties and makes decisions concerning the welfare of the child.

The Defendant or Respondent—In child welfare proceedings, one or both of the birthparents.

Witnesses—The individuals with information about a particular matter who are called to testify as to what they know.

Court Personnel—Individuals who work in the courtroom and who, along with the judge, facilitate the hearing of cases. Court personnel may include the bailiff, the minute clerk, and the sheriff's deputy.

During hearings, attorneys assist the judge in resolving disputes related to the well-being of a child. Attorneys often ask child welfare professional to present facts, in the form of evidence, to the court. Two types of evidence generally are used: written evidence and the testimony of witnesses. Written evidence may include documents prepared by the child welfare professional. As an example, at a hearing on termination of parental rights, an attorney might present a report prepared by a child welfare professional that describes the extent to which parents have complied with services and makes a recommendation on whether parental rights should be terminated.

Attorneys also often ask child welfare professionals to testify in court regarding the facts of a case. Their testimony may be required at a variety of hearings, which, depending on the state, may include:

Temporary Custody Hearings—Hearings in which the court determines whether the state is justified in taking immediate custody of the child. State law typically requires that this hearing occur within a short period of time after a child's removal from her parents' custody (such as 48 hours) to determine the child's placement.

Adjudication Hearings—Hearings in which the court determines whether the child is abused, neglected, or dependent.

Dispositional Hearings—Hearings that follow a finding of abuse or neglect during which the court determines who will become the guardian of the child and where the child will be placed.

Permanency Hearings—Hearings in which the court determines whether the permanency goal for the child is appropriate, given the alternatives, and whether current services are sufficient to ensure that the permanency goal will be achieved.

Parental Fitness Hearings—Hearings that determine whether a parent is a fit parent when the state has filed a petition to terminate parental rights and the parent contests the state's action.

Best Interests Hearings—Hearings that are held after a parental fitness hearing in which the court determines whether termination of parental rights is in the best interests of the child.

CHILD WELFARE PROFESSIONALS' RESPONSIBILITIES TO THE JUVENILE COURT

The Illinois *Code of Ethics for Child Welfare Professionals* describes the responsibilities of the child welfare professional to the juvenile court system as follows:

> Child welfare professionals should treat all parties to the case with respect, honesty, fairness, and cooperation.

> Child welfare professionals should thoroughly familiarize themselves with the background of the case involved.

> Child welfare professionals should testify honestly in court. They should apprise the court of all relevant facts in the case, both positive and negative, of which they are aware.

> Child welfare professionals should advise the court if they come to know of the falsehood of prior testimony given in a child welfare proceeding. Child welfare professionals should take appropriate action against any unethical conduct they observe in court.

These responsibilities can be summarized as the responsibilities to be fair, to be informed, and to be honest.

The Responsibility to Be Fair

The child welfare professional must be fair to all parties before the court, treating them with respect, honesty, fairness, and cooperation. The following case illustrates this responsibility:

> LaShauna is a private agency caseworker who is responsible for the case involving the Fredricks family. The family has a number of serious

problems. LaShauna recently discovered that Mr. Fredricks hit Mrs. Fredricks. LaShauna called the child abuse reporting hotline to report that she was fearful that the children were at risk of harm. The child protective services investigator, George, determined that the case was unfounded. LaShauna disagrees with George and has told him so. Subsequently, LaShauna and George are both called to testify in a matter involving another family.

LaShauna and George have a responsibility to put aside their differences about the Fredricks family and deal with the present case in an objective manner. Their professional responsibilities require them to treat one another with respect. Child welfare professionals often have repeated contacts with the parties at court proceedings: the judge, the attorneys, the birthparents, other witnesses, and the child. They may have had previous unpleasant encounters with some of these parties and may wish to avoid conversation with them. The child welfare professional, however, must put aside personal biases that may affect ongoing professional relationships with these individuals.

Being fair to the other parties in the courtroom supports proper decisionmaking. A judge is interested in the facts of the case so that he or she can make an informed decision. When a child welfare professional is not fair and respectful to other parties in the courtroom, her behavior presents a distraction to the court and interferes with the court's ability to make the best decisions. Such behavior may harm the clients that the child welfare professional is charged with helping.

The Responsibility to Be Informed

The child welfare professional also has the responsibility to be thoroughly informed about the background and the facts of the case before testifying. A professional should never testify if she has failed to read the case record. Before testifying, the professional should meet with the attorney who summoned her to testify to obtain a clear understanding of the information that should be presented.

When a child welfare professional testifies and does not have a thorough familiarity with all relevant facts of a case, he not only fails the client but the court as well. A court can make a decision based only on the facts before it, and in many cases, the child welfare professional is the only individual who can testify to certain facts contained in the case record. If the professional is not informed, the court is likely to be put in the position of making a decision based on incomplete information. The following case illustrates the professional's responsibility to be informed:

> Benton has had an extremely large caseload since he assumed responsibility for another 10 families when one of his coworkers left the agency.

One of the new families is the Xavier family. Benton simply has not had time to give the Xaviers his full attention. Benton is called to testify at the adjudicatory hearing. Before the hearing, he reviews the service plan, but he does not have time to read any of the previous caseworker's notes. Had he read the notes, he would have noted that the previous caseworker was suspicious that Mr. Xavier, the father, was abusing drugs and that the caseworker had recommended that Mr. Xavier be assessed for substance abuse. Benton testifies that he believes that the Xavier child should be returned home, and the court follows his recommendation.

In this case, Benton's failure to make himself aware of all relevant information led him to make a recommendation that could result in harm to a child for whom he has responsibility. He did not supply the court with the information that it needed to make the best decision.

Other problems can result when a professional testifies without complete information. A caseworker, for example, whose testimony during direct examination is based on incomplete information, may find that his mistakes are pointed out by opposing counsel during cross-examination. The caseworker's entire credibility, as a result, may be put into question, and the court may ignore even those aspects of his testimony that are knowledgeable and informed. The case example involving Benton may be taken a step further:

> The members of the Xavier family have undergone psychological evaluations, and the service plan prepared by the previous caseworker reflects the recommendations of the psychologists. When the state's attorney asks Benton what services would be required to protect the Xavier child from risk of harm, Benton testifies to the requirements of the service plan. Defense counsel then questions Benton about the various caseworker visits with the Xavier family, and Benton cannot respond to these questions. Defense counsel then asks Benton how he knows what services are required for the family. Benton replies, "Because they were included in the service plan prepared by the previous caseworker."

Although Benton's answer is accurate, it is hardly the best answer that Benton could have provided to help the court make the necessary decisions. It is correct that Benton accurately described the services that the Xavier family needed prior to the return of their child to them, but he could not tell the court the basis for his answers. The court, under such circumstances, may view his testimony less than favorably.

The Responsibility to Be Honest

All witnesses have an obligation to testify truthfully and can be found guilty of perjury (a criminal offense) if they lie under oath. Child welfare professionals have the responsibility to apprise the court of all relevant facts in the case, both positive and negative, of which they are aware. When professionals fail to testify fully and truthfully, they not only expose themselves to criminal liability, but they also fail to provide the court with the information needed to make the best decisions. The following case illustrates the responsibility to be honest:

> The state's attorney has called Brandy, a caseworker, to testify in a hearing to terminate parental rights. Brandy believes that the parents' rights should be terminated because the mother has failed to visit her child over the last 18 months. Brandy also knows that the mother has complied with all the tasks specified in the service plan.

In this case, Brandy must testify about both the mother's failure to visit her child and her compliance with the service plan. Even if the state's attorney does not inquire about the mother's participation in services, defense counsel will likely ask Brandy about the mother's efforts in this regard. Brandy must testify that the mother has complied with the tasks in the service plan or she may, in effect, be providing false information to the court.

The responsibility to be honest also extends to advising the court if the professional learns of a falsehood in prior testimony given in a child welfare proceeding. In many cases, witnesses in a proceeding are asked to leave the courtroom during the testimony of other witnesses and, therefore, the professional may not be aware of the nature of the testimony of others. In some cases, however, a child welfare professional may become aware that the court is proceeding on the basis of a substantial misconception. In such a case, the professional should speak with the attorney who is handling the matter. It is the attorney's responsibility to ensure that the testimony of all witnesses is true and accurate.

SUMMARY

Child welfare professionals frequently must participate in court proceedings and provide crucial information about the facts of a case. Child welfare professionals have the responsibility to their clients and to the court to be fair, informed, and honest. Fairness means, among other things, that child welfare professionals should make an effort to be aware of their own particular biases regarding clients, court personnel, and other child welfare professionals with whom they may have had previous dealings and put those feelings aside while testifying. Failure to maintain fairness and objectivity about the facts of a case may result in decisions that are detrimental to the child's best interest Likewise, the responsibility to be fully informed about the matters on which the professional is testifying is critical to the welfare of the child. Testifying on the basis of incomplete or incorrect information can not only mislead the court but also, when exposed, compromise the credibility of the profession also that even his or her well-grounded testimony is disregarded. Finally, honesty is critical to the court process. The role of the witness is to provide truthful and accurate information to the court, even when the professional fears to outcome of the information on the final outcome of the case. It is the responsibility of the court to weigh all testimony and evidence to determine the best outcome for the child.

CASE STUDIES FOR CHAPTER 7

Case Study 7-1. Darius just returned from vacation. While he was away, he was assigned a new case. He does not have the complete file, so he has called the previous caseworker to obtain additional information about the family. The previous caseworker sounds very judgmental and defensive about her work with the family. Darius does not have time to meet the family before the court date on Wednesday. What should Darius do?

Case Study 7-2. Darcy dislikes the state's attorneys. She has many preconceived ideas about them and avoids talking to them as much as possible. Could this be problematic for Darcy's clients?

Case Study 7-3. Eppie has been the caseworker for Ben for two years. Ben has a conduct disorder and is in need of intensive treatment for behavior problems. Eppie has not received a report from the residential treatment facility where Ben is placed, and a hearing is scheduled in one week regarding Ben's progress. Eppie has not seen Ben since the last hearing. She has not insisted upon a report because she believes that the treatment facility is responsible for Ben, and she has a great deal of other work to do. Is Eppie's approach acceptable?

Case Study 7-4. Catalina likes her client, Jenny, a great deal. The judge, however, does not like Jenny and is "fed up" with her. Catalina believes that the judge is unfair and is tempted to exaggerate some of the positive steps Jenny has taken. Would Catalina be justified in doing so?

Case Study 7-5. Milly is intimidated by lawyers. She always feels insecure and tongue-tied around them. Court hearings are scheduled for several of her cases over the next few weeks. Because of her discomfort with lawyers, she has avoided speaking with any of the attorneys for her clients. Should Milly avoid these conversations until the court dates?

Chapter 8

Termination and Transfer

Termination of services and transfer of cases are inevitable regardless of the service outcome. The means by which services are terminated and cases are transferred, however, significantly affects clients, both children and adults. Professionals must be sensitive to the processes they use to transfer cases and terminate services.

The Illinois *Code of Ethics for Child Welfare Professionals* provides the following with regard to the termination of services:

> Child welfare professionals should not abandon their clients. Child welfare professionals should continue appropriate intervention with clients until intervention is no longer required to meet the needs of the child or is no longer appropriate under the applicable statute. At that time, intervention is terminated.

> Child welfare professionals should promptly notify clients when termination or interruption of services is anticipated.

> Prior to termination, for whatever reason, except precise order of the court, child welfare professionals should provide appropriate pretermination counseling and take other steps to facilitate transfer of responsibility to another colleague or provider of services if further intervention is required.

> Child welfare professionals should request the transfer of a case to another professional when compelling reasons prevent successful professional intervention.

This chapter discusses the concepts of abandonment and continuity, outlines proper termination procedures, and offers recommendations for conducting responsible transfers of cases and termination of services.

ABANDONMENT AND CONTINUITY

The Illinois *Code of Ethics for Child Welfare Professionals* states that "child welfare professionals should not abandon their clients." The ethical requirement that prohibits client abandonment does not preclude a professional from terminating services or transferring cases, but it requires that services be terminated or cases transferred only under certain circumstances and only in certain ways. To abandon a client is to end services while the client is still entitled to receive them. Abandonment is incompatible with a key aspect of the competent delivery of child welfare services, continuity. Continuity includes continuity of care (that is, consistent, ongoing care without lapses in services to which the client is entitled) and continuity of relationships.

Children who lack continuity in their lives are deprived of the familiarity, sense of security, and predictability that are necessary for normal emotional and psychological development. A sense of security is possible when the environment is familiar and the course of events is predictable. Most children who are served by the child welfare system have been harmed by a lack of continuity in their lives before they enter the system.

They may have been exposed to environments with intermittent living arrangements, inconsistent schedules, and frequent changes in the adults in their lives. When children enter the child welfare system, they should be provided with stability and continuity, among other benefits. Children's placements, however, often are not stable and continuous. Caseworkers and/or foster parents may continually change, and children repeatedly may find themselves with unfamiliar people and in unfamiliar environments. They may feel unable to predict the course of events in their lives and may be left with a sense of insecurity and a mistrust of the adults around them.

Continuity is also important for adult clients. The child welfare system is complex, and clients may find themselves in unfamiliar situations and have difficulty predicting what will happen next. They are likely to feel unsure and fearful as they deal with the loss of their children and the complicated system they are required to navigate.

Child welfare professionals can provide some level of consistency in clients' lives through continuity in the services they provide. Simple ways to provide continuity include remaining in close contact with clients, informing clients of court dates, and clarifying for clients the conditions under which their children can be returned to them so that clients are not confused about expectations. The following examples illustrate a lapse in continuity:

> After a foster parent adopts a child in his care, he is uncertain of the services the child may continue to be entitled to receive and is unable to get in touch with his caseworker.

> A caseworker is offered a supervisory position at another agency. She notifies her supervisor and leaves the agency the following week without informing her clients.

A caseworker is assigned a case that previously was handled by another caseworker. He has difficulty determining how to proceed because the previous caseworker made only very sketchy case notes.

These scenarios illustrate instances in which termination of services or transfers of cases were handled poorly. In each situation, clients were left feeling abandoned because of a lapse in continuity.

Child welfare professionals routinely terminate services and transfer cases for a variety of justifiable reasons and do so in ways that do not threaten the continuity of services. Although it would be preferable for clients to be served by the same caseworker throughout the duration of services, caseworkers can maintain some degree of continuity by terminating services or transferring clients' cases in responsible ways. The following examples illustrate responsible processes:

A child is adopted by his foster parents. The caseworker provides a period of follow-up services to ensure a smooth transition and then terminates services.

A caseworker is told that she will be promoted to supervisor within the next few months. She immediately informs her clients that she will transfer their cases to other caseworkers. She meets with the new caseworkers to review her case notes and introduces the new caseworkers to her clients.

A caseworker believes that her client, a 16-year-old boy, is a threat to his foster family and to herself. On one occasion, the boy calls the caseworker's home and threatens her husband. After recommending that the boy be placed in a residential facility, the caseworker asks to be removed from the case. She provides the new service provider with the boy's complete case history

The two children of a young mother are removed from her care for about a year as a result of neglect. After she completes a drug rehabilitation program and parenting classes, she regains custody of her children. The caseworker continues to make regular visits for about six months and feels confident that the situation is stable. The judge shortly thereafter authorizes the closing of the case. The caseworker gives the mother her telephone number at the office and asks her to call if she needs assistance.

In each of these examples, the termination of services or the transfer of the case was handled appropriately. Clients were not abandoned, and transitions were smooth.

TERMINATION OF SERVICES AND THE CHILD'S BEST INTERESTS

It sometimes becomes necessary to terminate services to adult clients because the continuation of services is not in the child's best interests. This situation most commonly occurs when a parent is not progressing toward reunification or is not progressing quickly enough, and the child, as a result, may remain in foster care for a lengthy period of time. Although parents and other family members are considered clients, the primary responsibility of the child welfare professional is to the child. Parents and other family members are clients only to the extent that the provision of services to them is instrumental to ensuring the well-being of the child who has experienced abuse or neglect.

A child welfare professional must be prepared to change the permanency goal from a return home to adoption when further investment in the parent is contrary to a child's best interests. This decision often includes the termination of parental rights. Compassionate caseworkers who wish to see families reunited may become so focused on serving parents that they do not regularly assess progress from the viewpoint of the child's best interests. Child advocates frequently emphasize that a child's perception of time is very different from that of an adult, and that especially during early development, children need the permanency of family. The child's needs, consequently, may require terminating services to the parent. In addition, federal law mandates that permanency be achieved quickly for children in foster care. Parents must be informed that if they do not demonstrate sufficient progress toward reunification within certain time frames, they risk having their parental rights terminated.

GUIDELINES FOR ETHICAL TERMINATION OF SERVICES AND TRANSFER OF CASES

Social work ethicist Frederic Reamer (1988) suggests the following guidelines for ethical termination of services and transfer of cases by child welfare professionals:

> Keep accurate case notes so that when other caseworkers assume responsibility for cases, they are fully informed of what has taken place.

> Give clients as much advance notice as possible when services are being terminated or their cases are being transferred.

> Remain in contact with the client throughout services.

> When terminating services, leave clients with telephone numbers and addresses of resources that they may need.

In cases involving discharge of clients from a residential facility, develop a comprehensive discharge plan, notify significant others of the client's discharge, and advise the client of the notification to significant others.

Follow up with clients for whom services have been terminated.

Carefully document in case records all decisions and actions related to termination of services.

Consult with colleagues and supervisors about any decision to terminate services or transfer a case. When possible, prevent the need to terminate services or transfer a case by addressing the relevant issues. (As an example, when a foster parent and a child in her care are having difficulties, steps should be taken to resolve the problems whenever possible instead of moving the child to another foster home.)

SUMMARY

Child welfare professionals have the responsibility to provide continuity and to refrain from abandoning clients. Termination of services and transfer of cases are inevitable aspects of child welfare services. Child welfare professionals, however, should strive to maintain continuity of care by notifying clients before any change occurs, providing appropriate pretransfer counseling, ensuring that clients receive the services to which they are entitled, and organizing case records for the professional who assumes responsibility.

Child welfare professionals also must be prepared to terminate services with parents when doing so is in the best interest of the child.

CASE STUDIES FOR CHAPTER 8

Case Study 8-1. Kia, a caseworker, has grown tired of her job and finally has been able to secure a new job in another agency. She is very happy about the new position and is so eager to leave her current job that she tells her new employer she can begin the following week. She realizes that she is not giving proper notice to her current employer. She nonetheless, does not return telephone calls, misses appointments, and calls in sick for several days so she can take advantage of accrued sick leave and can shop for new work clothes. What will be the effect of Kia's behavior on her clients?

Case Study 8-2. Martha is a well-respected caseworker but puts off writing up case notes as long as possible because she dislikes paperwork. She is at least four months behind on her case notes when she is killed in an automobile accident. What problems of continuity does this present for her former clients?

Case Study 8-3. Tina is the caseworker for LaTanya, age three. LaTanya has been in foster care for one year, and her permanency hearing is approaching. LaTanya's foster parents want to adopt her, and LaTanya is thriving in their home. LaTanya's mother, LaTisa, uses cocaine and currently is participating in a residential treatment program. Although she has relapsed several times, she continues to express a desire to regain custody of LaTanya, and she seldom misses a visit with her. What should Tina recommend to the court in terms of termination?

Case Study 8-4. Carlos, a 9-year-old Spanish-speaking child in foster care, was sexually abused as a very young child. Until recently, Carlos seemed to doing well in the Jimenez foster home. Unaware of Carlos' history of sexual abuse, the Jimenez family has been uncertain how to respond to his recent, mildly inappropriate sexual behavior. When the foster family becomes aware of Carlos's history, they ask the agency to remove him from their home because they are concerned about the safety of their biological children. Unable to find a suitable foster home for Carlos, the agency places him in the Theta Residential Facility, a center intended for very sexually aggressive children. When the residential facility realizes that Carlos will need a Spanish-speaking therapist, Carlos is transferred to another of its facilities. Dr. Fernandez is assigned Carlos' case and as she prepares to begin his therapy, she reviews his case records and realizes that he is not an appropriate candidate for the therapy provided at that facility. Moreover, in her opinion, the Theta Residential Facility is not an appropriate placement for Carlos. Upon Dr. Fernandez's recommendation, plans are made to transfer Carlos to a different type of facility. Could Carlos's caseworker have prevented the multiple transfers that Carlos has experienced?

Chapter 9

When Others Act Unethically

What should a child welfare professional do when ethics and ethical decisionmaking mean less to colleagues than to the professional? This uncomfortable situation can occur when a professional discovers that a coworker has been engaging in what appears to be unethical conduct or a supervisor tells the professional to follow an agency policy that the professional believes may ethically cause a problem for a client. This chapter discusses how child welfare professionals who discover ethical misconduct by coworkers or who find that they are working in an unethical environment can address these dilemmas.

IDENTIFYING THE PROBLEM

Child welfare professionals have an obligation to follow ethical standards of conduct and make decisions that respect the interests of all the parties involved. When child welfare professionals ignore ethical principles, there are consequences for clients, the caseworker, the agency, and the profession. A child welfare caseworker who fails to respect confidentiality may cause harm to a family. She may find that her credibility and integrity are called into question in court. When the ethical transgression is severe, the media may learn of the situation and publicly berate the child welfare agency, leading to public distrust of child welfare professionals in general.

Child welfare professionals who strive to integrate ethical standards into their professional conduct and who find that they are working with others who disregard those standards may react in different ways. In one case, they remain committed to ethical practice and find themselves at odds with others, including their supervisors, who do not have compunction about ethical principles. Alternatively, they may be tempted to abandon their allegiance to ethical standards in order to "fit in" at their agencies. As discussed in Chapter 2, an employee more easily maintains integrity when the work environment supports ethical behavior. Similarly, when the environment does not support ethical behavior, it is more likely that professionals will find it harder to adhere to ethical constraints on their behavior. They may begin to believe that it is acceptable to take ethical "shortcuts."

ETHICAL VIOLATIONS BY COWORKERS

When professionals observe others failing to adhere to ethical standards, they must consider what steps they should take to address the situation. The professional should ask two questions: Has my co-worker worker committed an ethical violation? What should I do at this point to protect clients? Admittedly, there are no easy answers to these questions, but there are guidelines that may be useful.

1. DO NOT JUMP TO CONCLUSIONS.

   A child welfare professional should be careful not to jump to conclusions about the conduct of coworkers. It is possible that an initial observation is accurate, and that a coworker is not concerned about ethical principles. It is also possible that, although certain conduct appears to be an ethical violation, it is not.

   A caseworker, for example, who is required to put in eight-hour days may sign out at noon every day, stating that she will visit clients. She also may describe to a coworker the matinee movies she has seen recently. A coworker may jump to the conclusion that her colleague is signing out early to see afternoon movies. It is possible that the caseworker has been spending extra time with her clients, taking them to movies after school and conducting home visits after 5:00 P.M., or that she sees afternoon movies on weekends.

2. GET THE FACTS.

   When a professional is seriously concerned that a coworker may be violating an ethical standard, the best strategy is to discuss the situation with the coworker. The information that the coworker provides can provide a logical explanation for what appears to be an ethical violation. Although a direct conversation may be uncomfortable, it is one of the easiest ways to obtain needed information to resolve the question of a potential ethical violation. Taking a less direct route may create additional problems. If a professional, for example, reviews her coworker's client files and the coworker learns of this activity, the coworker may complain that client confidentiality has been violated or her own privacy intruded upon.

   When speaking to a coworker about such a sensitive matter, the professional should consider the coworker's personality and avoid confrontations and accusations. Such statements as the following are appropriate: "I want to talk to you about something I have seen recently;" "I am not making any accusations;" and "I want to talk to you about this, instead of going to others in the office first." The professional may find that her coworker is not aware of certain ethical principles that apply to the situation at hand. The coworker may be grateful that the problem has been identified and a solution found.

3. DO NOT GOSSIP.

Gossip is the indiscriminate sharing of information about alleged conduct of another. When a professional observes a potential ethical violation, there is the temptation to talk with others in the office to confirm that they, too, believe that the observed conduct appears to be an ethical violation. This approach is usually a bad idea because it creates the risk that false information about a coworker will be spread through the office. If a professional believes that she must consult another individual about the matter, the best strategy is to approach one's supervisor. If, however, the professional has a specific reason for consulting with another individual in the office, the discussion should be a consultation and not a gossip session. A consultation is a private discussion with a coworker regarding a potentially problematic situation. There is a distinction between consulting with another individual and spreading gossip. Gossip takes place among a number of people; a consultation is a private discussion. Gossip has, at its intent, the spread of information; consultation has, as its intent, obtaining advice. Gossip takes place among indiscriminately selected individuals; consultation takes place with a trusted person. The following openings to conversation illustrate the differences between gossip and consultation:

> **#1:** Hi, Carlos. Look, there's something I really need to talk about and I'd appreciate it if you kept it between us for right now. I need your help with something I have seen and I'd really like it if you would give me some advice. The other day, I saw Ben reach into the petty cash drawer without leaving a receipt for the money he took. I know that Ben has been assigned a family with seven children and that the children's father was recently hurt in an accident. However, I also know that Ben has been having his own financial problems. What should I do?

> **#2:** Hi, Carlos. Hey, Marty. Hey, did you hear about Ben? From what I hear, his wife has a gambling problem, and they're drowning in debt. Of course, I've also heard that she has a prescription drug addition. That must run into some bucks. The other day, I saw Ben taking money out of the petty cash drawer without leaving a receipt. I can't help but wonder if he hasn't taken the money for himself, although I do know that he's been dealing with a family with seven kids and the father just lost his leg in an accident. Do you think he took it for himself?

In the first situation, the caseworker is seeking consultation, that is, the advice of a colleague. The caseworker did not mention unnecessary matters (such as rumors about Ben's wife), and the tone is not malicious. In the second situation, however, the speaker clearly gives the impression that he is conveying the information to harm another person's reputation. He does not seek advice regarding how he should handle the situation. The tone is much more malicious, and the speaker relies more on speculation than facts.

4. CONSULT A SUPERVISOR.

The professional's supervisor is in the best position to address ethical problems connected with coworkers' conduct. The supervisor also is in the best position to assist the professional in sorting through the issues and deciding whether an ethical violation exists. A professional always should include her supervisor in determining her response to a potential ethical violation on the part of a coworker. Talking with a supervisor about a coworker's potential ethical violation, however, may be considered "whistle-blowing," and some professionals may attempt to avoid getting involved because of the potential ramifications. This issue is discussed in greater detail later in this chapter.

ETHICAL VIOLATIONS IN THE WORK ENVIRONMENT

Although observing ethical violations by coworkers can present problems, it is frequently an issue that can be resolved quickly. More complicated situations arise when a child welfare professional discovers that her work environment does not support ethical decision-making. This can happen in a number of ways:

> Phillipe is a caseworker in the Zeta Child Care Agency. Phillipe overhears Bertha, the administrator of the agency, speaking with a new employee, Marsha. Bertha tells Marsha, "Here is a copy of the agency's code of ethics. You might find it useful at some point, although I have never once opened it since I took over two years ago."

This type of attitude on the part of an administrator can permeate an entire agency. Soon, none of the employees may consider ethical behavior a priority.

> Phillipe is a caseworker in the Zeta Child Care Agency. Bertha, the administrator of the agency, has begun dating George. The new boyfriend has two children from a previous marriage and was involved in a fierce custody battle with his ex-wife. Phillipe watches as one day Bertha decides to run a criminal record and a child abuse record check on George's ex-wife. Bertha tells Phillipe, "I hope I can find something juicy on her. It would help George out a lot and I would score some serious points with him."

This type of conduct suggests that the agency does not consider ethical standards to be very important. In the face of such conduct on the part of an administrator, the professional should consider whether the work environment as a whole is an ethical one.

The following list provides some of the options that a professional may consider, depending on the type of ethical issue she confronts in her work environment:

- Speak with your immediate supervisor.

- Speak with a person whom you believe sets an ethical standard of conduct.

- Determine whether there is an ethics committee at the agency and if so, speak with a member of the committee.

- Raise the issue at a staff meeting.

- Make a conscious commitment to adhere to ethical standards, document the ethical decisions you make that conflict with the decisions that others in the organization may have made, and note the sources you consulted to reach that decision.

- Seek another position where the environment is more ethical.

WHISTLE-BLOWING

Once a professional determines that another individual in the agency has violated an ethical standard, she should first determine whether the issue can be resolved informally, and if not, she should refer it to appropriate superiors and/or to the ethics committee of the agency. Whistle-blowing is the reporting of an ethical violation to authorities. Whistle-blowing should be considered only after a child welfare professional very carefully reviews the situation at hand and confirms that a serious ethical transgression has occurred or will occur. The following example illustrates the type of situation that may lead to whistle-blowing:

> Duncan works for the Delta Foster Care Agency. After working for the agency for six months, he concludes that the agency regularly engages in unethical practices. Duncan finds another job, but before leaving, he witnesses the Delta agency director submit fraudulent reimbursement forms to the public child welfare agency. Duncan decides to call the state's Office of the Inspector General to discuss his concerns and report the incident.

In this case, the Delta Foster Care Agency was defrauding the public child welfare agency and possibly harming the agency's clients. Duncan's decision to contact the

Office of the Inspector General was correct because it provides the public agency with an opportunity to rectify ethical (and possibly legal) violations.

Whistle-blowing is not appropriate in every case and should not be taken lightly. If a professional engages in whistle-blowing irresponsibly, she can cause irreparable harm to the agency and the persons who are the subject of the report. When considering whether whistle-blowing is necessary, the professional should ask herself five questions:

1. Is there adequate evidence that misconduct has occurred?
2. How serious is the ethical violation (that is, what is the degree of harm)?
3. How likely is the harm?
4. Have all internal options been exhausted?
5. How likely is it that whistle-blowing will rectify the ethical violation?

The following example illustrates the decisionmaking process:

> Carol is a therapist at the Yeta Child Welfare Agency. Carol is aware that on several occasions, the agency director, Ms. Jones, has made decisions that have put children at risk. In some cases, Carol has been able to intervene and convince Ms. Jones to take another course of action. Carol has wondered about Ms. Jones' credentials. The diploma on her office wall is from a school that is unknown to Carol, and although the diploma states that Ms. Jones has a Ph.D. in counseling, Carol notices that Ms. Jones is apparently unaware of several fundamental principles of counseling that Carol herself learned in graduate school. On a hunch, Carol makes a few telephone calls and learns that the school from which Ms. Jones graduated is not accredited. Carol does not want to leave Yeta. She is concerned that the children the agency serves are at risk. Ms. Jones, however, has begun to make it quite clear that she does not appreciate Carol's interfering in her management of the agency.

First, Carol should ask whether she has adequate evidence that Ms. Jones is incompetent. She is fairly certain that Ms. Jones does not have appropriate credentials to manage the agency. She knows that Ms. Jones' degree is not from an accredited school. She and Ms. Jones have disagreed on certain cases, which may demonstrate Ms. Jones' lack of clinical competence. Carol might consider conferring with agency staff who hold MSW degrees regarding the differences of opinion she has had with Ms. Jones to determine how other professionals view Ms. Jones' clinical competence.

Second, Carol should ask whether there is a risk of harm to clients or others. Carol has witnessed Ms. Jones putting children at risk of harm on several occasions because she has exercised poor clinical judgment.

Third, Carol should assess whether additional harm is likely to occur in the future. Based on the regularity with which Ms. Jones has made poor decisions in the past, Carol might safely predict that the of risk harm to children is likely to continue.

Fourth, has Carol exhausted her internal options? She has spoken with Ms. Jones on a number of occasions about the decisions that she has made that have put children at risk of harm. Because Ms. Jones is the agency director and Carol's supervisor, Carol cannot turn to another administrator in the agency. Finally, will whistle-blowing effectively address the problem? Because the agency has a contract with the public child welfare agency, whistle-blowing through notifying the public agency may result in an investigation and a decision by the public child welfare agency to discontinue the contract with Yeta so that children are not put at risk of harm. In sum, this case provides a good example of a situation in which whistle-blowing should be considered seriously.

SUMMARY

Child welfare professionals sometimes suspect that a colleague is acting unethically. Although there is a positive duty to take steps to address a colleague's unethical behavior, the professional should proceed carefully. First, without gossiping or making accusations, the professional should get the facts by raising the concern with the person whose conduct appears unethical. this approach should be as diplomatic as possible and should take into account the colleague's personality and temperament.

If raising the issue with the individual is not a viable option or does not prove successful, the professional should bring her concerns to her supervisor. the supervisor would then take over responsibility for investigating and addressing the conduct involved. In some circumstances, such as when unethical behavior involves the senior administrators at an agency, it may be necessary to alert outside authorities. this is often called "whistle-blowing." Because whistle-blowing is a drastic step which may have negative impacts on both the agency and the reporter, it should be considered only as a last resort when the potential harm to clients or the public is serious and probable and feasible internal solutions have been exhausted.

CASE STUDIES FOR CHAPTER 9

Case Study 9-1. Mary Kay has been working as a case manager at the Zeta Child Care Agency for six months. She recently discovered that one of the foster families will be moving and wants the child in their care to remain with them. Mary Kay calls the licensing representative and explains that the family has helped the child to make significant progress. She asks if there are forms that the family must complete because they are moving and how to arrange for an inspection of their new home. The licensing representative responds, "Oh, that rule about applying for a new license every time a family moves is just an administrative nuisance. Don't worry about filing out a new application or arranging for an inspection. If no one is aware that they've moved, there's no chance that the placement will be interrupted." How should Mary Kay respond?

Case Study 9-2. Johnson shares an office with Kim. One day, Johnson overhears Kim soliciting a bribe from a client. What should Johnson do?

Case Study 9-3. Tiana, a new caseworker at the Epsilon Agency, just completed a class in ethics for child welfare professionals. On numerous occasions, she made references to the ethical principles that were discussed in her class. Her coworkers have been ignoring her. One day when walking by the lunchroom, Tiana hears two coworkers chatting. One says, "That Tiana is such a pain. She is a little Miss Goody-Two-Shoes. Does she really think she can change the way we do things here? I've been here five years, and I know how to do my job. I don't need to hear about 'ethics,' especially from a fresh 23-year-old." What should Tiana do?

Case Study 9-4. Katie's desk is located next to JT's desk at the Xena Foster Care Agency. Katie is offended by the lewd remarks that JT makes when he is flirting on the telephone with his girlfriend, Cheryl. Katie has tried to ignore this behavior. Recently, she has become suspicious that JT's girlfriend is one of his clients, Cheryl Smith. Last week, she saw JT holding Cheryl's hand in the office. What should Katie do?

Case Study 9-5. Pedro is concerned that his coworker, Lucy, is drinking too much. He is hesitant to mention it to Lucy because he does not want to offend her. He also does not want to discuss his concerns with others in the office because gossip is rampant. He does not want to tell their supervisor because he does not want to get Lucy in trouble. Nevertheless, Pedro is fairly certain Lucy is an alcoholic, and he is concerned about her and the way she is serving her clients. What should Pedro do?

Case Study 9-6. Danielle does not like her supervisor, Mel, at the Yap Agency. Mel can be very controlling. She scrutinizes every step that Danielle takes. Recently, Mel approved Danielle's recommendation of a return home goal for the Smith children. Unfortunately, some information about the Smith family that was in the public agency's file was not forwarded to the Yap Agency when the family was referred to the agency. At the permanency hearing, the judge, who is very familiar with the Smiths, chastises Danielle for her recommendation and makes a comment that the work at the Yap Agency is not responsibly handled. A reporter hears about the judge's comments and calls Mel for a comment. Mel blames Danielle's poor casework. The story runs on the front page of the paper's Metro section. Danielle is very angry and wants to report Mel to someone. Is this whistle-blowing? What should Danielle do?

References

Beauchamp, T. L., & Childress, J. F. (1989). *Principles of biomedical ethics.* New York: Oxford University Press.

Davis, M. (1997). Developing and using cases to teach practical ethics. *Teaching Philosophy, 20,* 374–375.

Gambrill, E., & Gibbs, L. (2002). Making practical decisions: Is what's good for the goose good for the gander? *Research on Social Work Practice, 4*(1), 31–46.

Kennedy, N. J., & Sanborn, J. S. (1992). Tardive dyskinesia is an irreversible neurological condition characterized by involuntary muscular movements. *Pharmacy Bulletin, 28*(1), 93–100.

Lidz, C. W., Meisel, A., Zerubavel, E., Carter, M., Sestak, R. M., & Roth, L. H. (1984). *Informed consent: A study of decision making in psychiatry.* New York: Guilford.

MacDonald, G. (2000). *Effective interventions for child abuse and neglect: An evidence-based approach to planning and evaluating interventions.* New York: John Wiley & Sons.

O'Donohue, W., Fisher, J. E., & Plaud, J. J. (1989). What is a good treatment decision? The client's perspective. *Professional Psychology: Research and Practice, 20,* 404–407.

Ozar, D., & Sokol, D. (1994). *Dental ethics at Chairside: Professional principles and practical applications.* St. Louis: Mosby-Year Book, Inc.

Reamer, F. G. (1990). *Ethical dilemmas in social service* (2nd ed.). New York: Columbia University Press.

Reamer, F. G. (1998). *Ethical standards in social work: A critical review of the NASW code of ethics.* Washington, DC: NASW Press.

Rooner, R. (1992). *Strategies for working with involuntary clients.* New York: Columbia University Press.

Sactrett, D. L., Richardson, W. S., Rosenberg, W., & Haynes, R. B. (1997). *Evidence-based medicine: How to practice and teach EBM.* New York: Churchill-Livingston.

Glossary of Terms

Abandonment. Termination of services to a client who continues to be entitled to services.

Absolute right. A right that cannot be taken away or overridden, such as a child's right to be protected from abuse.

Abuse of power. The use of one's professional position for personal gain.

Accountability. Responsibility for the provision of services that are most likely to help clients achieve desired outcomes, the evaluation of client progress on an ongoing basis using valid measures, and the sharing of the results with clients.

Actual conflict of interest. A situation that arises when a child welfare professional, entrusted to exercise objective judgment in the service of an agency and its clients, has an interest that could interfere with the objectivity of that judgment.

Adjudication hearing. A court hearing which determines whether a child is abused, neglected or dependent.

Apparent conflict of interest. A situation which does not necessarily involve a potential or actual conflict but which causes a person, unaware of the complete facts of the situation, to reasonably infer that a conflict exists.

Attorney. A person who represents a party before the court.

Audit. The systematic, critical appraisal of the quality of services, including the procedures used for assessment and intervention and the resulting outcomes for clients.

Bar attorney. The term used in some jurisdictions to refer to an attorney who represents one defendant before the court when there are two defendants and a need for two defense attorneys in order to prevent a conflict of interest.

Best interest hearing. A court hearing that takes place in some states after the parental fitness hearing to determine whether termination of parental rights would be in the best interest of the child.

Breach of confidentiality. A professional's disclosure of personal information about a client that the client has good reason to believe will be kept in confidence.

Character. The desire and willingness to practice in accordance with professed values.

Code of ethics. A document that articulates the values of a profession and sets the guidelines and boundaries for professional conduct.

Coercion. Limiting a client's choices in order to force the client to agree to a preferred alternative.

Cognitive capacity. The ability to receive, process, and assimilate information.

Competence. The requisite ability to carry out one's professional responsibilities; also refers to a client's capacity to make his own decisions.

Confidentiality. The ethical value favoring the protection of information shared within the professional-client relationship.

Conflict of interest. A situation in which a child welfare professional, entrusted to exercise objective judgment in the service of an agency and its clients, has an interest that could interfere with the objectivity of his judgment.

Confirmation bias. Acceptance of only that information that supports one's preferred views while ignoring counter-evidence.

Consultation. A private discussion focused on ways to handle a potentially problematic situation.

Continuity of care. Consistent, ongoing care without lapses in services to which the client is entitled.

Court personnel. Individuals who work in the courtroom and handle court matters. Court personnel may include the bailiff, the minute clerk, or the sheriff's deputy.

Criterion referenced. Informed by information related to specific outcomes.

Defense counsel. The attorney who defends a party before the court.

Dilution effect. The result of failing to provide a service as intended in "full strength" form. A dilution effect may occur when services are reduced because of time constraints, limited resources, lack of client cooperation, or limitations on staff training.

Disclosure. With respect to a conflict of interest, the communication of the interest to relevant parties.

Dispositional hearing. A hearing in some states held after a finding of abuse or neglect to decide who will serve as guardian for the child and where the child will be placed.

Divestment. With respect to a conflict of interest, the disposal of the conflicting interest.

Duty to warn. The obligation of a professional to warn another of potential harm.

Ethical decision-making. The process of evaluating ethically relevant considerations in choosing a course of action.

Ethical standards test. The evaluation of ethical rightness through the use of a set of ethical standards and values.

Evidence-based decisionmaking. The conscientious, explicit, and judicious use of current best evidence in making decisions.

Exercise of judgment. Decision-making guided by expertise rather than by rules.

Fiduciary relationship. A relationship between a professional and a client that is dependent on the client's trust in the professional.

Gossip. Indiscriminate sharing of information about the alleged conduct of a person.

Guardian ad litem (GAL). An advocate for the best interest of the child who is independent of the parents and the state. Depending on the jurisdiction, the GAL may or may not be a lawyer.

Informed consent. The ethical requirement to advise clients of the probable outcomes of the alternatives before they agree to participate in any treatment or program.

Integration (stage of assessment). The review of all the information gathered about a client to make an assessment about the problem at hand and the potential solutions.

Integrity. The integration of an individual's values into his character and the making of ethical choices as a result.

Interest. An obligation, loyalty, responsibility, duty, or desire.

Judge. The individual who hears evidence and arguments in court. The judge makes decisions on the issues presented concerning the welfare of the child.

Limits of confidentiality. The point at which a professional can no longer maintain confidentiality.

Manipulation. Offering choices to a client in such a way that the client is led to select a particular option.

Multiple relationships. A situation in which a professional has a nonprofessional relationship with an individual for whom he is expected to make professional decisions.

Negative right. A right that requires that others refrain from interfering.

Outcomes test. The evaluation of ethical rightness based on the benefit that an action will produce.

Parental fitness hearing. A court hearing held in some states in situations in which the state has moved to terminate parental rights and the parent contests.

Particular right. A right that applies to a specific person in a specific situation.

Permanency hearing. A court hearing to determine the appropriate permanency goal for a child in foster care.

Positive right. A right that requires others to take affirmative action to meet an individual's specific need.

Potential conflict of interest. A situation in which there is no existing conflict of interest but there is some likelihood that the situation will change and the individual will have an interest which could reasonably be expected to affect future decision-making.

Procedural fidelity. The match between how a method should be implemented for maximal effect and how it is actually implemented.

Psychosocial factors. Aspects of a person's developmental history, personal history, and present environment that influence the individual's behavior.

Qualified right. A right that can be overridden.

Rationing. The restriction of the supply of a good or service by explicit or implicit means when demand exceeds supply and market mechanisms do not create an adequate supply to meet the level of demand.

Reasonable person standard. The standard that requires a professional to provide the information that a reasonable person would want to know before consenting (or withholding consent) regarding participation in a particular service or program.

Recusal. The diffusion of an ongoing conflict of interest by withdrawing from the decision-making process when a conflict situation occurs.

Reflective ability. The ability to identify the values at stake among many possible courses of action and to determine the choice that best manifests the individual's professional values.

Respondent. The term used in some jurisdictions to refer to the person against whom charges have been filed in court. The respondent (often also referred to as the defendant) often is one or both of the birthparents.

Right. An entitlement which creates a corresponding responsibility for others either to act in a certain way or to refrain from interfering with the holder of the entitlement.

Self-determination. The capacity to determine the course of one's life through the choices he makes.

Social validity. The community acceptability of intervention goals and methods in light of their intended and unintended effects.

Task-specific capacity. The level of client competence relative to a particular task.

Temporary custody hearing. A court hearing held in some jurisdictions to determine whether the state is justified in taking immediate custody of the child. It is typically held within a short period of time (such as 48 hours) after the removal of a child from her parents' custody.

Triage. The process of assigning priority based on the extent to which services, funds and resources can be best used or are most needed.

Universal right. A right to which everyone is entitled.

Value. A desirable quality, condition, or practice.

Voluntary choice. Making a decision without coercion or manipulation.

Whistle-blowing. The reporting of an ethical violation to authorities.

Witness. An individual who has information about a matter and is called to testify about the matter in court.

About the Authors

This book was authored by the ethics staff of the Office of Inspector General of the Illinois Department of Children & Family Services ("OIG") in a project funded by the University of Chicago School of Social Service Administration.

Project Supervisors

Denise Kane, who received her Ph.D. in social work from the University of Chicago, is the Inspector General for the Illinois Department of Children & Family Services

Elsie Pinkston, who received her Ph.D. in developmental and child psychology from the University of Kansas, is a professor at the University of Chicago School of Social Service Administration.

Authors

Martin Leever, who received his Ph.D. in philosophy from Loyola University of Chicago, was a member of the OIG Ethics Staff from 1997–2000 and is currently an assistant professor at the University of Detroit–Mercy.

Gina DeCiani, who received her J.D. from the University of Illinois Law School, is coauthor of *Legal Ethics for Paralegals and the Law Office* and has been a member of the OIG Ethics staff since 1998.

Ellen Mulaney, who received her J.D. from Yale Law School, served as a member of the Illinois State Board of Ethics from 1986–1996, and has been a member of the OIG Ethics Staff since 1994.

Heather Hasslinger, who received her A.M. in social work from the University of Chicago, was a member of the OIG Ethics Staff from 1999–2000 and is currently a member of the Parenting Assessment Team at the University of Illinois–Chicago.

In conjunction with:

Eileen Gambrill, who received her Ph.D. in social work and psychology from the University of Michigan, is Hutto Patterson Professor of Social Welfare, University of California at Berkeley.